Advanced Player's Guide

JÄRNRINGEN:

Martin Grip, Mattias Johnsson, Mattias Lilja

LEAD DESIGNER:
Mattias Lilja

GRAPHIC DESIGN:
Johan Nohr

CONTRIBUTIONS:
Mattias Johnsson
Anders Lekberg

PROOFREADING:
Brandon Bowling

ILLUSTRATIONS:
Martin Grip

PRINT:
Spindulio spaustuvė
Kaunas, Lithuania 2016

A VERY SPECIAL THANKS TO:

Paul Baldowski, Jocke Bergström, Babak Bobby, Brandon Bowling, Lars G Bäckström,
Martin Ekberg, Linus Eklund Adolphsson, Martin Englund , Aline Gladh,
Ulrika Haake, Garry Harper, Martin Hägg, Dan Kallin, Martin Kallin, Petra Kallin,
Martin Larsson, Adam Lindersson, Andreas Marklund, John Marron, Magnus Muhr
and our friends over at Rollspel.nu and /r/symbaroum

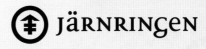

Symbaroum   **JÄRNRINGEN**

VERSION:	ISBN:	COPYRIGHT:
1.0.2	978-91-87915-20-8	Nya Järnringen AB 2016

The act of creation

IN THE WORLD OF SYMBAROUM people talk about the three primal forces Wyrhta, Wielda and Wratha; we were affected by them all as we finalized the Swedish *Core Rulebook* in the summer of 2014. Every act of creation is as much about harnessing as about creating; in order to complete a design one must destroy that which does not fit the mold; *"kill your darlings,"* as the expression goes. The great thing about roleplaying games is that the act of creation goes ever on.

As soon as *Symbaroum* found its way into the hands of its players we received wishes, ideas and suggestions on alternative rules and new areas to develop. These, together with an array of resurrected darlings, constitute the basis of the *Advanced Player's Guide*. We hope that you will find having your characters walk the more obscure paths of Davokar as joyful as we found it penning them down.

Happy Gaming!

TEAM JÄRNRINGEN

THE CHARACTER

THE SKILLS

THE TOOLS

Welcome to the Advanced Player's Guide

THE WORLD OF Symbaroum provides a lot of options for players, and even if the *Core Rulebook* introduced a long list of occupations, races and abilities it only scratched the surface. This book reaches deeper, offers more contrasts and nuances, gives more alternatives for both characters and non-player characters.

THIS FIRST CHAPTER presents these new alternatives in broad strokes, while the rest of the book is divided into three sections called *The Character, The Skills* and *The Tools*. The first two sections describe the many new options in more detail - races, traits, abilities, powers and so on, that in different ways contribute to expanding a player's options when creating and developing his or her character.

The third section starts off with a chapter describing alternative rules - some directly relevant to the new races, occupations and abilities covered in earlier chapters, others which are of a more optional type, intended for gaming groups that want to add more complexity to the game mechanics. Finally there are two chapters that

expand on the players' ability to provide their characters with personalized equipment.

As always, the gaming experience is everything; should you for some reason want to tweak the rules and guidelines presented in this book, speak to your gaming friends about it. So called "house rules" are, and have always been, a central ingredient in what makes roleplaying the world's greatest hobby and form of entertainment.

ARCHETYPES & OCCUPATIONS (PAGE 10)
One new archetype is introduces with the *Advanced Player's Guide*, the Hunter. Previously it was embedded in the archetype Rogue, but it certainly deserves some special attention. For example, hunters differ

from rogues in terms of combat techniques – the former keeps at a distance while the latter engages in melee. Additionally, while the hunter specializes in stalking their prey and putting down fleeing enemies, the actions of the rogue are more closely linked to treasure-hunting and mere survival.

Another addition is that all archetypes have been provided with an Archetypical Ability; a feature that captures the essence of the archetype. Not everyone walking the path of a particular archetype learns this ability, but many do and all would likely benefit from doing so.

In regards to occupations, Symbaroum's game world contains a multitude of professionals and the *Advanced Player's Guide* offers the players more examples, to use directly or as inspiration. Many are closely linked to the powerful factions of Ambria and Davokar, and are hence best suited for players who are already familiar with the game world. Nothing prevents a player from using these occupations when creating their first character, but if doing so they should also read up on relevant sections in the *Core Rulebook*, to learn more about how their particular faction (and its adversaries) regards the world – since one can assume that the character is knowledgeable about such things.

Furthermore, the *Advanced Player's Guide* introduces Professions. It takes a lot to become a member of a profession, both in terms of abilities and in accepting the worldview and ambitions such membership entails. Normally, it is not possible to start as the member of a profession; becoming one takes more *Experience* than what new characters are awarded. Instead, professions are something to aim for in the long run.

RACES (PAGE 38)

The *Advanced Player's Guide* features five new races: elf, abducted human, dwarf, troll and undead. Aside from providing players with additional options to create the character they want to play, these five races offer unique entries into the world of *Symbaroum*. The changelings, ogres and goblins of the *Core Rulebook* are tied to the world but tend to be outsiders – much like a player new to the game, their knowledge of the world is limited. Elves, dwarves and trolls belong to the old races of the world and if you opt to play as one of them you are expected to know quite a lot about Davokar and its surroundings; as you would if you had played *Symbaroum* for a while. Of course, you can play an elf who has not been tutored by his elders, a dwarf who has not listened to his patriarch or a troll who

Making House Rules

The option to create your own house rules is one of many things separating roleplaying games from other interactive media. This creative process is highly encouraged by Team Järnringen, since we very much like to see you make *Symbaroum* your own.

We tend to make house rules ourselves, at the following levels:

- **Alter presentation:** We change the esthetics more often than the actual rule. If the way an ability or power is enacted does not suit the player's idea of his or her character, the presentation is changed without altering the rule itself. Here the player's freedom is considerable, since the balance of the mechanics is not affected. For example, an independent mystic may spray acid instead of fire with his or her Brimstone Cascade. And an ogre may use its stone-hard lower arm to parry and tackle its enemies, in combination with the Shield Fighter ability.
- **New abilities:** If an ability seems to be missing, we create it. In fact, many abilities in the game derive from such player-driven initiatives. However, in these cases the group must be involved so that the balance of the game is maintained.

has slept through the educational songs. But in general, as a player of one of these races you would do well to study the campaign material in the *Core Rulebook* intensely.

Abducted humans are individuals taken by the elves in exchange for a baby changeling, and their fate constitutes a quaint mix of fighting for the elven cause in Davokar and feeling linked to the world of humans. All abductees normally know a lot about the world and its major conflicts, at least in terms of how they are regarded by the Iron Pact.

Undead, in the form they appear here, as a playable race, are a relatively recent phenomenon in Symbaroum's world. Previously encountered undead are thoroughly corrupt and ravenous, but members of the playable race Undead are not necessarily damaged to such an extent. To be sure, the player character has awoken to life after death, showing signs of having died yet still walking the land. This bitter fate means that the undead character is marked and hunted, likely darkened in mind without yet being entirely corrupted by darkness.

TRAITS (PAGE 48)

The races covered by this book have their own traits to exhibit their characteristics and role in the world. Also, note that when using the *Advanced Player's Guide*, some of the *Core Rulebook*'s traits are transformed into Boons and Burdens. These traits function like they did before and the races that previously had them from the start are now granted the corresponding boon or burden for free.

BOONS AND BURDENS (PAGE 50)

Boons is a new category, even if it existed implicitly in the *Core Rulebook*: the traits *Contacts* and *Bushcraft* now become boons instead. Boons are more limited in their use than abilities and more suited for problem-solving when compared to the combat-oriented abilities. The boons are also perfect for adding nuance to a player character, for a lesser cost in *Experience* points. Any character can acquire any boon; it is most often a question of practice. But since they tend to be associated with certain cultures and environments we offer some suggestions regarding which occupations they are best suited for.

A system of burdens is also presented in this book, for gaming groups that enjoy such a concept. In fact, the trait *Pariah* in the *Core Rulebook* is here counted among the burdens. Burdens are characteristics, phenomena or repercussions of life-choices which make life harder for the character – but more interesting for the player. When adding burdens to their characters from start, the players gain a few more *Experience* points to use when selecting abilities and powers. In other words, the burdens allow for players and gaming groups to create characters with diverse life experiences; for instance, older characters can be designed using added *Experience* points but burdened by a traumatic past or damaging life-choices.

ABILITIES (PAGE 60)

The abilities and powers introduced in the *Advanced Player's Guide* are closely related to the new occupations. However, even if linked to a specific occupation most abilities can be selected by anyone, just like the *Core Rulebook* abilities.

Exceptions from this rule are the abilities which define Professions and Archetypes. Sure, in theory these abilities may have been passed on to a character by some dissident, or exist in similar forms within other factions or groups. The recommendation is that the gaming group decides together whether to use the restricted abilities as they are presented in the *Advanced*

Archetypical Abilities

For a character to count as a member of an archetype and be eligible to choose its ability, he or she must have at least three of the abilities listed in the description of the archetype. In this case, having the novice level of the abilities is enough.

Player's Guide or if they should be available to any and all characters. A mix of these is possible, but risks damaging the thrill for players who are striving towards a Profession.

The gaming group can regard the Archetypical abilities in the same ways: either as something available for all (in essence, disconnecting them from the archetypes) or as skills only accessible to player characters belonging to a specific archetype. Hence, we would suggest that the players and Game Master sit down to discuss how to deal with Professions and Archetypical abilities in play. After all, the world of *Symbaroum* is yours and you decide what makes it exciting and fun!

MYSTICAL TRADITIONS (PAGE 74)

The traditions presented in the *Core Rulebook – Sorcery, Theurgy, Witchcraft* and *Wizardry* – are dominant in Ambria and Davokar, but they are not alone in teaching mystical powers to those wanting to learn. The *Advanced Player's Guide* presents three more traditions and a new mystical practice.

From Clan Vajvod's territory in eastern Davokar come the Symbolists: rune-crafters and symbol-carvers knowledgeable about the grand design of the world. Ominous signs and dark omens attract symbolists to Ambria and deep into Davokar, searching to decipher the world's destiny.

From their mythical underground realm come the Troll Singers: skalds and storytellers with enchanting voices. Something is terribly wrong in the harmonies of the world, and for some trolls this continuous disharmony is reason enough to travel the surface.

Out of the depths of Davokar come the Staff Mages, stern warrior monks claiming to descend from the Emperor's Guard of Symbaroum. From their castle, hidden deep within the forest, these ascetics have fought an uneven fight for redemption ever since the fall of the empire. The Staff Mages are powerful, but the power of their enemy grows faster and the mages travel south in the hunt for allies and apprentices.

The elves of the Iron Pact have long been under tremendous pressure and few points of light shine in their dark skies. However, in recent years, help has come from an unexpected source: the Artifact Crafters among the trolls have started to share their secrets, awakening an all but forgotten mystical practice. Allegedly, abducted humans tend to be welcomed by the trolls. Ordo Magica has also acquired the knowledge to infuse mystical powers into craft-items and it is rumored that they strive to have at least one skilled Artifact Crafter in each of their chapters.

POWERS & RITUALS (PAGE 78)

The *Advanced Player's Guide* introduces lots of new mystical powers, both for the established traditions and the new ones: *Staff Magic, Symbolism* and *Troll Singing*. Exactly like in the *Core Rulebook*, anyone can learn any power, but the mystic is only protected from corruption when learning and using the powers included in a tradition he or she belongs to.

ALTERNATIVE RULES (PAGE 98)

The *Advanced Player's Guide* presents a list of new abilities which need clear and expanded rules to work as intended. Adding to that, this book provides a number of optional rules for the gaming group to consider. All these are assembled in the rules chapter.

EQUIPMENT (PAGE 110)

Just like in the *Core Rulebook*, a character is from the start awarded the weapons and equipment related to its selected abilities, plus a dagger. Aside from that, the character starts with 5 thaler, unless stated otherwise by boons or burdens.

Table 1: Starting Equipment

ABILITY/POWER	EQUIPMENT
Agile Combat	Longbow
Armored Mystic	Medium Armor
Arrow Jab	Optional ordinary ranged weapon
Axe Artist	Optional ordinary axe, single-handed or heavy
Blacksmith	Optional ordinary weapon and Medium Armor (made by the character)
Flailer	Optional Jointed Weapon
Hammer Rhythm	Optional hammer, single-handed or heavy
Knife-play	Stiletto
Man-at-arms	Medium Armor
Polearm Mastery	Spear or Staff
Pyrotechnics	An alchemical grenade and a dose Flash Powder
Rapid Fire	Optional ordinary ranged weapon
Shield Fighter	Shield
Staff Fighting	Optional ordinary Long weapon
Staff Magic	Rune Staff
Steel Throw	A throwing weapon
Sword Saint	Ambrian Fencing Sword or Estoc, plus a Parrying Dagger
Symbolism	Protective Symbol
Troll Singing	Skald's Cuirass
Twin Attack	One ordinary single-handed weapon (novice), two ordinary single-handed weapons (adept)
Two-handed Force	Optional ordinary heavy weapon
Witch Hammer	Optional ordinary single-handed weapon

he group huddled in a booth at the back of the smoky tavern. Despite the ominous atmosphere, Jela felt like laughing at the scene. Kasimer almost ended up in the lap of Arron, and it was hard to tell whether the dwarf or the abductee was more uncomfortable. Too big for the booth, the troll Gormyx sat on the floor. Even sitting he was taller than the others, with horns that rose above their heads. His massive body served to screen them all from the rest of the room.

Their prospective mission-giver sat on a stool at the far end of the table, shrouded in a cloak and with eyes that glittered from within the deep hood. *"She is... different,"* Agneisha had said. The staff mage's aptitude for laconic understatements never failed; a weak scent of formaldehyde surrounded the skinny woman whose voice sometimes died out while she was speaking, as if she had forgotten to breath between one word and the next.

"I have two demands," the woman hissed. *"First: the false theurg must die. And second: you have to ... take me along for the journey."*

No one protested, but Kasimer coughed his voice to life: *"Maybe not my business to ask really, but what's your name? And what do you want with the priest?"*

She gave the dwarf a stern glare. *"You can call me Sarli."* After a short pause she added: *"The priest... will die... because he murdered me."*

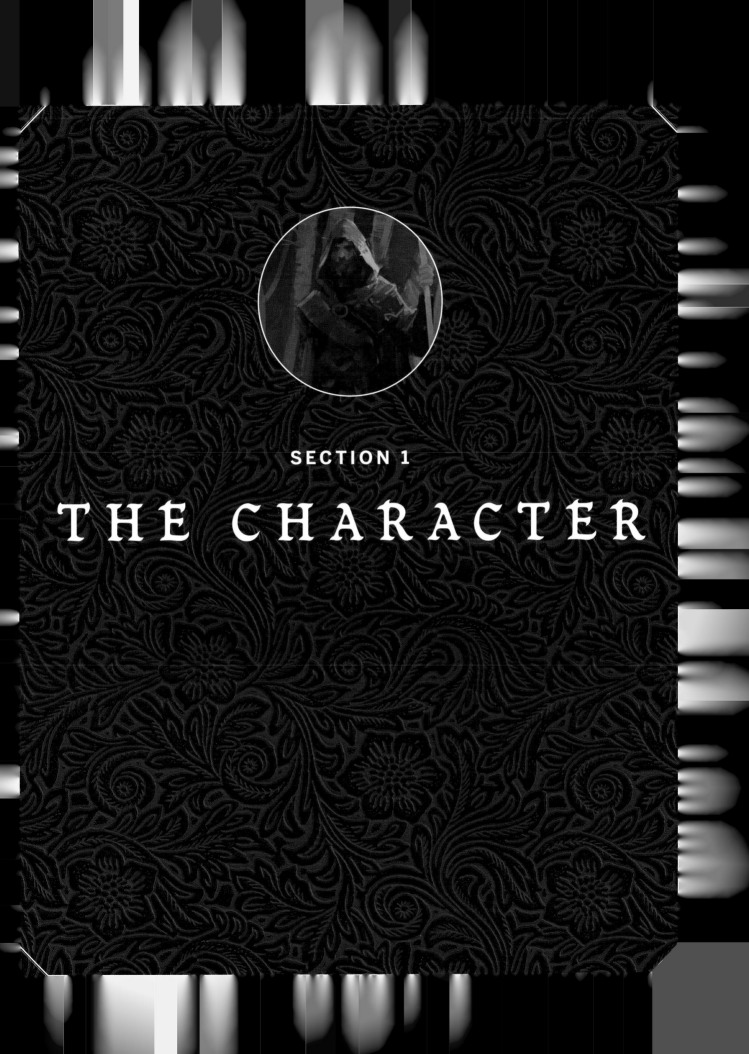

SECTION 1

THE CHARACTER

Archetypes

THIS CHAPTER DESCRIBES a number of occupations which make full use of all new abilities and powers. Moreover, a brand new archetype is introduced, the Hunter. Hunters were previously featured as a sub-group among the rogues, but there is hardly any doubt that they deserve to be recognized as an archetype in their own right.

Hunter

THE HUNTERS AND their toil are of great importance, both for the Ambrians and among the clans of the forest. To commoners in Ambria, they may not appear to be any different from your average rogue, but for many (especially among those living close to Davokar) they are on par with true heroes. Covered in the dirt of the wilds, eyes shining with the light of the future, the hunters are vital in the project of cultivating and taming the great forest.

Among both Ambrians and barbarians, the hunters are often signified by their skillful use of ranged weapons and techniques. Exactly how they fight is primarily decided based on what they are hunting: criminals, monsters or dark-minded sorcerers. But no matter the target, what unites the hunters is a highly developed sense for where the prey has been, how it moves and to where it is headed – a sense that with near supernatural precision is captured by the archetypical ability they all may learn, called *Hunter's Instinct*.

HUNTERS AND THE RACES
All races have their hunters, but in general it is primarily elves, abducted humans and humans

> ## Professions
>
> Some occupations listed in the *Advanced Player's Guide* are Professions, having tough requirements for membership. You cannot belong to such an occupation from the start – to be eligible for a profession the character must have all the abilities mentioned under Required Abilities, one of them at the master level. Professions are meant to be used as a character's goal, something to strive towards and plan for. Also, note that each profession gives access to a unique ability.

that excel in the area. Still, in Thistle Hold you may very well come across goblins and even a few ogres known as trustworthy guides through the wilds. Dwarves are seldom hunters in the forest, but some of Ambria's most widely known bounty hunters are dwarves who for some reason have left their families in Yndaros.

HUNTER ATTRIBUTES

Hunters are known to have keen senses (*Vigilant*) and be light on their feet (*Discreet*), as well as fast and agile (*Quick*). More versatile hunters have developed a skill to use just about any kind of weapon (*Accurate*), but a majority tends to use some single type of ranged weapon, maybe complemented by traps or poison (*Cunning*).

HUNTER ABILITIES

The following abilities include those listed in both the *Core Rulebook* and the *Advanced Player's Guide*, sorted according to attributes when relevant.

- **Archetypical ability:** *Hunter's Instinct* (three other abilities from below are required for this ability to be available)
- **Accurate:** *Arrow Jab, Marksman, Polearm Mastery, Staff Fighting, Steel Throw, Twin Attack*
- **Cunning:** *Alchemy, Beast Lore, Blacksmith, Loremaster, Medicus, Poisoner, Tactician, Trapper*
- **Persuasive:** *Dominate, Leader*
- **Quick:** *Acrobatics, Quick Draw, Rapid Fire*
- **Resolute:** *Bodyguard, Steadfast*
- **Strong:** *Iron Fist*
- **Vigilant:** *Sixth Sense, Witchsight*
- **General:** *Equestrian, Exceptional Attribute, Man-at-arms, Recovery, Ritualist*

HUNTER PROFESSIONS

Hunters can aim to become Iron Sworn, meaning a full member of the Iron Pact dedicated to hunting abominations and those who risk awakening the dark of Davokar.

Hunter Occupations

From among the occupations in the *Core Rulebook*, Witchhunter and Ranger count as hunters and not as rogues, which should be noted in regards to the archetypical abilities. In other words, characters who are Witchhunters or Rangers may learn the archetypical ability *Hunter's Instinct* if they are so inclined.

IRON SWORN (PROFESSION)
"Nevermore!"

The work of the Iron Pact is never done, which places great demands on its agents, the Iron Sworn. The pact was created by elves at the time of Symbaroum's downfall, and after a long time in the shadows its members are on the move again, trying to stop the spreading darkness. Davokar must never awaken, not if the Iron Sworn can help it.

Nowadays, the Iron Pact recruits new agents from all races and cultures; anyone sympathetic to the struggle is tested in a series of both physical and moral challenges. Those who make it with both life and loyalty intact are invited to swear the Iron Oath. After that follows a time of training and further testing before initiates become true members of the Pact – agents devoted to the fight against corruption.

- **Important Attributes:** *Accurate 13+, Quick 11+*
- **Suggested Race:** All
- **Required Abilities:** *Beast Lore, Loremaster, Marksman, Polearm Mastery or Twin Attack*
- **Unique Ability:** *Agile Combat*
- **Suggested Boons:** *Beast Tongue, Bloodhound, Bushcraft, Contacts, Enduring March, Pet*
- **Suggested Burdens:** *Bloodthirst, Nightmares*

BOUNTY HUNTER

*"Scum, me? Sure, but scum you need,
by the sound of it."*

During The Great War there were deserters – many doubted that a victory over the Dark Lords was possible. To deal with the problem, King Ynedar, Queen Korinthias's father, placed a permanent bounty on the heads of the runaways. In doing so, he indirectly founded the guild of the Bounty Hunters. The tradition to pay for having fugitives caught lives on and nowadays the bounty hunters are often forced to venture into the forest of Davokar, where the most desperate – and also most valuable – targets tend to seek refuge.

- **Important Attributes:** *Accurate 13+, Vigilant 11+*
- **Suggested Race:** Human, Dwarf
- **Appropriate Abilities:** *Cheap Shot, Ensnare, Marksman*
- **Suggested Boons:** *Bloodhound, Bushcraft, Contacts, Enduring March, Pack-mule, Telltale*
- **Suggested Burdens:** *Code of Honor, Impulsive*

Bounties

The following bounties can be collected in Ambria for a number of more or less common crimes. This only pertains to the bounty set by the Town Watch or equivalent; private bounties may also be posted by victims or their relatives. These private contributions can double and sometimes even increase a bounty by a factor of five or ten – making that particular target a much coveted prize!

Table 2: Bounties

CRIME	BOUNTY
Pick-pocket	1 orteg
Cat-burglar	1 shilling
Notorious burglar	1 thaler
Murderer	10 thaler
Mass Murderer	50 thaler
Cultist	10 thaler
Sorcerer	100 thaler
Spy	500 thaler
Deserter	10 thaler

MONSTER HUNTER

"Let me deal with your... problem."

As more and more Ambrians settle down in the shadow of Davokar, it grows more common that these settlements are haunted by the famished, vindictive or even life-hating horrors of the forest. In light of this growing threat, actionable individuals have developed techniques and skills for hunting monsters – the often considerable price of monster trophies is certainly another incentive! Also the barbarian clans have their monster hunters, even though the people of the forest adhere to the witches' taboos and seldom live or travel in monster infested areas.

A majority of the Ambrian monster hunters are members of monster hunting societies, established in or around places like Thistle Hold and Kastor. These groups both compete and cooperate in the never ending work to keep the border settlements secure and the members of the societies rich. The latter part, the wealth, has attracted a growing number of barbarian monster hunters south, where they have turned into very successful trophy collectors, thanks to their vast knowledge of Davokar.

- **Important Attributes:** *Cunning 13+, Accurate 11+*
- **Suggested Race:** Human
- **Appropriate Abilities:** *Beast Lore, Marksman* or *Polearm Mastery, Trapper*
- **Suggested Boons:** *Bloodhound, Bushcraft, Cartographer, Contacts, Pack-mule, Privileged, Servant*
- **Suggested Burdens:** *Addiction, Arch Enemy*

Monster Hunting Societies

In Thistle Hold, the monster hunters have gathered into a number of Societies, out of which The Red Claw is the most famous one. Other monster hunters of note are the boastful newcomers Markas' Impalers, and the more serious teratologists belonging to Nikanor's Taxidermian Guild, who collect monster carcasses in good condition for study purposes. Many of these groups have openly established outposts close to Karvosti and frequently visit the newly opened store Crueljaws' Traps, where the retired ogre who has given the establishment its name sells his ingenious hunting devices.

Warrior

ANYONE CAN TAKE UP arms against the authorities, those who are better off or to loyally protect their lord. Constant war and conflicts have led to the emergence of military orders and groups characterized by combat skills and lifestyles that mirror their worldviews. The *Advanced Player's Guide* introduces a number of new warrior occupations; they are all unique examples of how the constant of war has fostered the development of skills, community and institutions in both Ambria and Davokar.

The templar knights may be seen as the ultimate expression of how submission can lead to extraordinary power. Karvosti's Wrath Guards serve their High Chieftain, but some say they really fight and die for each other, for their brothers and sisters in blood, rather than for some higher purpose. Eastern Davokar is home to rune covered warriors, their flesh a tapestry of carved tattoos that summarizes the Symbolists' knowledge of war. There are also strong warrior traditions among trolls and elves – the rune smiths of the trolls wield their hammers as effectively on the battlefield as in the smithy, while abducted humans often utilize a spear dance as deadly as it is old.

The most pronounced characteristic of these warriors is something they all have in common: they must rise to the challenge, or fall. This quality is captured by the archetypical ability *Feat of Strength*.

WARRIORS AND THE RACES

Of the races presented in the *Advanced Player's Guide*, primarily abducted humans and trolls are regarded as great warriors. The trolls, with a culture based on physical challenges, are known to have bred many warriors. The aggressive, hot-headed abductees often serve the same purpose among their new families in the woods. Also, the undead may very well have a history full of violence – a possible explanation for their state of undeath.

WARRIOR ABILITIES

The following abilities include those listed in both the *Core Rulebook* and the *Advanced Player's Guide*, sorted according to attributes when relevant.

- **Archetypical ability:** *Feat of Strength* (three other abilities from below are required for this ability to be available)

- **Accurate:** *Hammer Rhythm, Polearm Mastery, Shield Fighter, Staff Fighting, Twin Attack, Two-handed Force*
- **Persuasive:** *Dominate, Leader*
- **Quick:** *Acrobatics, Quick Draw*
- **Resolute:** *Bodyguard, Steadfast*
- **Strong:** *Iron Fist*
- **General:** *Axe Artist, Berserker, Equestrian, Exceptional Attribute, Flailer, Man-at-arms, Opportunist, Recovery, Rune Tattoo, Sword Saint*

TEMPLAR (PROFESSION)
"For Prios, the One!"

The church of Prios and its representatives are protected by the Knights of the Dying Sun, heavily armed and with the fire of faith burning behind their breastplates. The power of faith makes the armor of the sun knights harder than steel. Their mere presence repels abominations by the sheer radiance of their conviction or by weapons burning with Prios' holy rage.

Lately, a schism is said to have grown between the commander of the templars and the church's Curia in Templewall. Initially, the dispute was about how to handle the ancient sun temple found close to Karvosti, but apparently there are other ideological differences between the Knights of the Dying Sun and that of the Sun Church in general.

What will come of this conflict is not easily guessed; some dismiss it as a natural effect of the church's development, others whisper of a possible division of the church, in line with the conflicting views that exist regarding the dying Prios and humanity's role in the drama.

- **Important Attributes:** *Strong 13+, Resolute 11+*
- **Suggested Race:** Ambrian
- **Required Abilities:** *Iron Fist, Man-at-arms, Mystical Power (Witchhammer)* or *Mystical Power (Holy Aura), Theurgy*
- **Unique Ability:** *Armored Mystic*
- **Suggested Boons:** *Commanding Voice, Contacts, Enterprise, Heirloom, Privileged, Servant*
- **Suggested Burdens:** *Code of Honor, Dark Secret*

TATTOOED WARRIOR

"My anger burns on my body; come closer, feel the heat!"

Many barbarian warriors have their bodies covered with tattoos, but the tattooed warriors of Vajvod differ in that they are tattooed by Symbolists – mystics with a special understanding of the power of symbols. The foremost among the tattooed warriors serve as the guards of Clan Vajvod's chieftain.

There are also goblins and trolls among the tattooed warriors, totally unrelated to the work of Vajvod's Symbolists. Amid both trolls and goblins, these warriors comprise an elite among the elite. The tattooed warriors are often seen fighting alongside their ruler on the field of battle, be it down in the Underworld or in the shadowy depths of Davokar.

- ◆ **Important Attributes:** *Strong 13+, Quick 11+*
- ◆ **Suggested Race:** Barbarian, Goblin, Troll
- ◆ **Appropriate Abilities:** *Iron Fist, Rune Tattoo, Polearm Mastery* or *Two-handed Force*
- ◆ **Suggested Boons:** *Bushcraft, Enduring March, Horrifying, Tough*
- ◆ **Suggested Burdens:** *Dark Secret, Impulsive*

RUNE SMITH

"The rhythm of the world echoes in the beat of my hammer."

Among the trolls there are warriors who have sworn a holy oath to only fight with weapons of their own making, dressed in armor crafted by their own massive hands. These rune smiths count among the most skilled craftsmen of the Underworld and are fierce warriors. It seems ogres are also drawn to the fire of creation, just as elves appreciate the art of the forge, the hammer often held by abducted humans.

In Ambria, there are strong blacksmith traditions but even if blacksmiths are often seen wielding their own weapons, most of them lack the dedication the trolls show on the battlefield. However, lately the old secrets have begun spreading to Ambria, lifting its blacksmiths to new heights.

- **Important Attributes:** *Strong 13+, Cunning 11+*
- **Suggested Race:** Abducted Human, Ogre, Troll
- **Appropriate Abilities:** *Blacksmith, Hammer Rhythm or Two-handed Force, Iron Fist*
- **Suggested Boons:** *Contacts, Enduring March, Forbidden Knowledge, Heirloom, Pack-mule*
- **Suggested Burdens:** *Mystical Mark, Protégé*

WEAPON MASTER

"You want to live, I want to die and be remembered in awe."

Among the warriors of Ambria and Davokar there are those who have committed themselves to becoming true masters of a specific weapon. Through persistent training, these weapon masters have become very skilled with their weapon of choice, and often adhere to a philosophy about the struggle between life and death.

They are known as Sword Saints in Ambria, devoted to perfecting their skill with the chosen weapon. Among barbarians there are the Axe Artists, often wielding one axe in each hand – a tradition also adopted by some of the goblin tribes of Davokar. The Elven equivalent to a weapon master is called a Spear Dancer, an art form also practiced by abducted humans. Among trolls, chain weapons are considered extra noble, both very demanding and very effective in the right hands. Such Flailers, in the form of ogres, can often be found in the gladiatorial arenas of Ambria.

- **Important Attributes:** *Accurate 13+, Quick 11+*
- **Suggested Race:**
  Sword Saint: Ambrian, Changeling
  Flailer: Ogre, Troll
  Spear Dancer: Abducted Human, Elf
  Axe Artist: Barbarian, Goblin
- **Appropriate Abilities:**
  Sword Saint: *Acrobatics, Man-at-arms, Sword Saint*
  Flailer: *Flailer, Ensnare, Two-handed Force*
  Spear Dancer: *Acrobatics, Staff Fighting, Polearm Mastery or Ensnare (if using a Chain Staff)*
  Axe Artist: *Axe Artist, Acrobatics, Twin Attack*
- **Suggested Boons:** *Commanding Voice, Contacts, Gambler, Heirloom, Privileged, Servant, Tough*
- **Suggested Burdens:** *Arch Enemy, Code of Honor*

WRATH GUARD (PROFESSION)
"I bleed, you die."

The High Chieftain of Karvosti is guarded by a select number of warriors in the Guard of the Slumbering Wrath. Anyone who has met a wrath guard in combat knows that there is nothing drowsy about them. On the contrary, the blood of a wrath guard is boiling with fighting spirit, and the Huldra teaches them to use that passion effectively. To damage a wrath guard is to wake its fury; to badly hurt an experienced guard is like summoning a furious aboar in human shrouding.

Every clan sends their nine most skilled warriors to Karvosti to become members of the Wrath Guard. Nominations are made by the clan chieftains when one of their representatives falls in combat or – in singular cases – retires. He or she who is appointed can hardly say no, partly because the mission is regarded as one of the most honorable a clan warrior can be tasked with, partly because a rejection likely would mean exclusion from the clan or see the warrior branded as an outlaw. There are tales of barbarians who have been appointed to the wrath guard after having left their clans, and therefore refused to serve. But it is also said that the defiance of these defectors always ends up costing them their lives, sooner or later...

- **Important Attributes:** *Strong 13+, Resolute 11+*
- **Suggested Race:** Barbarian
- **Required Abilities:** *Iron Fist, Man-at-arms, Recovery, Shield Fighter or Twin Attack*
- **Other Requirements:** Barbarian human
- **Unique Ability:** *Blood Combat*
- **Suggested Boons:** *Blood Ties, Bushcraft, Enduring March, Heirloom, Pack-mule*
- **Suggested Burdens:** *Bestial, Bloodthirst*

Mystic

THE WORLD OF SYMBAROUM is vast and marvelous, and many are the mystic traditions that have come and gone throughout history. Aside from the more widespread traditions, there are more obscure ones rooted in the forest – the Symbolists who supersede the witches in authority within Clan Vajvod, the ascetic Staff Mages deep inside Davokar and the Troll Singers, common among trolls and elves. Then there are the Artifact Crafters, mystics who instill power into artifacts of the lower order, rather than casting spells or performing rituals.

It should also be noted that there are subcultures within the established traditions, here called Specializations. The witches have their Paths, the wizards their Schools, the theurgs two Roads and sorcerers can focus on a Domain.

Amongst the witches there are those who devote themselves to walking only one of the paths, referred to as Blood Waders, Green Weavers or Spiritualists. In the wizardry tradition there has long existed three currents focused on the mysteries of fire, the senses and the will. Schools have formed around these mysteries, known as Pyromancy, Illusionism and Mentalism. A wizard is not required to choose a school but it is considered a merit to do so. Actually, in the larger chapters of Ordo Magica, where the competition for power and influence is most intense, membership in one of the schools can prove valuable as it may give access to benevolent colleagues and mentors.

The theurgs of the Law Giver are faced with a different question: are you meant to be a combatant of darkness or a caretaker of the light? Not all theurgs chose one or the other, instead balancing these contradictory perspectives all their lives. However, most take a stand and accept their purpose knowing that other champions of the light will make a different choice and see that the balance of faith is maintained.

Sorcery is likely as old as the oldest of the other traditions. Its representatives usually have to operate in secret, which is why they have a hard time communicating and sharing their knowledge with each other. In spite of this, two distinct undercurrents have developed in the form of the Death Mages, commonly known as Necromancers, and the abominable Demonologists who subdue and bargain with abominations and other monstrosities from the Yonderworld.

All these specializations count as professions, meaning that they require more from their practitioners than other occupations do, but also give access to unique abilities. Irrespective of path, school, road or domain, all mystics are grounded in the will to understand and control their surroundings – a dream made more reachable by the archetypical ability *Strong Gift*.

MYSTICS AND THE RACES

Of the new races introduced in the *Advanced Player's Guide*, primarily elves, trolls and the undead are associated with mystical powers; *Witchcraft* and *Troll Singing* is common among elves and trolls, and the grim fate of the undead may very well have been caused by the individual's own mystical practices.

Furthermore, the trolls have their renowned artifact crafters and blacksmiths, and also abducted humans sometimes master these arts, trained by trolls who have seen fit to help their old allies, the elves.

MYSTIC ABILITIES

The following abilities include those listed in both the *Core Rulebook* and the *Advanced Player's Guide*, sorted according to attributes when relevant.

- **Archetypical Ability:** *Strong Gift* (three other abilities from below are required for this ability to be available)
- **Accurate:** *Natural Warrior, Polearm Mastery*
- **Cunning:** *Alchemy, Beast Lore, Blacksmith, Loremaster, Medicus*
- **Persuasive:** *Dominate, Leader*
- **Quick:** *Acrobatics*
- **Resolute:** *Mystical Power, Steadfast*
- **Strong:** *Steadfast*
- **Vigilant:** *Sixth Sense, Witchsight*
- **General:** *Berserker, Exceptional Attribute, Recovery, Ritualist, Staff Magic, Symbolism, Theurgy, Troll Singing, Witchcraft, Wizardry*

ARTIFACT CRAFTER (PROFESSION)
"My soul is at one with my crafts."

The making of artifacts is a highly sought-after art form that for a long time was lost to elves and humans. However, among the trolls it has been kept alive, as an almost sacred practice. Lately, the knowledge has been revived by humans and elves, in both cases thanks to the trolls of Davokar. The elves received it as a gift from a former ally, to aid them in these dark days, but how Ordo Magica managed to get their hands on the lost art is not known. However it happened, the knowledge has spread so that every chapter soon will have at least one artifact crafter in its service.

- **Important Attributes:** *Cunning 13+, Resolute 11+*
- **Suggested Race:** Abducted Human, Ambrian, Elf or Troll
- **Required Abilities:** *Blacksmith, Loremaster, Mystical Power (optional), Ritualist*
- **Unique Ability:** *Artifact Crafting*
- **Suggested Boons:** *Archivist, Contacts, Enterprise, Forbidden Knowledge, Heirloom*
- **Suggested Burdens:** *Elderly, Protégé*

Artifact Crafting in Ordo Magica

The sudden reemergence of artifact crafting among wizards has made others question the source of the knowledge. One belief is that the Ambrian mystics have stolen it from the trolls – maybe even captured and tortured a troll – while others suspect that the rulers of the Underworld have traded this gift in exchange for something very valuable. What version lays closest to the truth is not easily guessed and the Grand Master refuses to speak on the topic.

STAFF MAGE (PROFESSION)
"My staff is my soul and my weapon."

The mystics called Staff Mages have gotten their epithet from the rune covered staffs they always carry. A rune staff is an expression of the staff mage's strength as well as a powerful weapon – something that has led to some wizards of Ordo Magica calling them by degrading names like *"Wand-throwers"* or *"Broomsticks."* To the staff mage, the staff is an extension of his or her soul and to experienced staff mages it may sometimes be difficult to tell where the mage ends and the staff begins; they are part of the same whole.

Whatever you call them, the staff mages are said to descend from an order of warrior monks, tasked with protecting Symbaroum's last emperor. After the fall of Symbaroum, they withdrew to their castle deep inside Davokar. It was not until recent times that they became known to the people of the south; before that they only sought new recruits among the northern barbarian clans – individuals suited for an ascetic life in the shadow of death. Many of the potentials tended to be changelings.

With the darkness spreading through Davokar, the staff mages have expanded their area of search to include the southerners and their realm. Hence, the plainly dressed warrior monks with their characteristic rune staffs can sometimes be seen visiting Ambria's duchies and courts, hunting for novices and allies in the fight against the horrors haunting the ruins of Symbaroum.

- **Important Attributes:** *Resolute 13+, Cunning 11+*
- **Suggested Race:** Barbarian or Changeling.
- **Required Abilities:** *Loremaster, Mystical Power* (optional), *Polearm Mastery, Staff Fighting*
- **Other Requirements:** Permanent Corruption 3 or less
- **Unique Abilities:** *Mystical Power (Staff Projectile), Staff Magic, Ritualist (Blood Storm* and *Quake)*
- **Suggested Boons:** *Archivist, Bushcraft, Commanding Voice, Enduring March, Horrifying, Servant*
- **Suggested Burdens:** *Code of Honor, Protégé*

SYMBOLIST

"I paint and the world obeys."

That symbols and signs have power is well-known and made use of in most mystical traditions, at least in rituals. Pure Symbolism is a tradition that almost solely builds its power on symbols and signs.

It came to Davokar with mystics from the east who, after having fled across the Ravens, found a sanctuary in the river lands that later became the territory of Clan Vajvod. Ambrian scholars suspect that Symbolism – strange, powerful and decadent – is a vital clue to understanding why the barbarians of eastern Davokar are in disagreement with Karvosti and its authorities, the Huldra and the High Cheiftain. It may lead to an explanation as to why the Vajvods, for cultural and philosophical reasons, distance themselves from Karvosti, and at the same time, are more open to outsiders than other clans, Clan Odaiova excluded. Rumor has it that Vajvod's Clan Chieftain, Zoltar the Old, has not a witch but a symbolist by his side, likely one trained at the Azure Temple in the heart of the river lands.

- **Important Attributes:** *Resolute 13+, Cunning 11+*
- **Suggested Race:** Barbarian (Clan Vajvod), Goblin, Troll
- **Appropriate Abilities:** *Mystical Power (usually Protective Runes), Ritualist (usually Carve Rune Tattoo), Symbolism*
- **Suggested Boons:** *Archivist, Augur, Cartographer, Contacts, Heirloom*
- **Suggested Burdens:** *Elderly, Mystical Mark*

Other Worlds and the Origin of Humans

FOLKLORE IS FULL of tales of other worlds, parallel to the physical world that is the home of the living. Some of these myths also speak of the origin of humankind and there is a worrying pattern to the tales, a pattern indicating that humans stem from somewhere else; stuff of legend which has been granted support by the enormous stone ships found stranded in the far east, beyond the Ravens and the desert where a human empire – sometimes talked about as the First Empire – is said to have blossomed and died. From whence the humans once came to this world is not known, but the existence of other worlds is more or less an established fact, at least among scholars.

For mystics and others studying the subject there is no doubt that this world is only one of many. There have been attempts to establish a verifiable classification and one of the most talked about is Katrandama's Triptych, named after a sorcerer who was burned to death in Kadizar in approximately year –24. Katrandama left notes and drawings behind regarding the composition of the world.

Before her, most mystics believed the cosmos to be divided in two: the world of the living, and an un-world inhabited by spirits and abominations. Katrandama crushed this dichotomous worldview and imagined that the worlds fitted together as the pieces of a three-part altarpiece, with the physical world in the middle and the wings made up of the Spirit World and the Yonderworld. Normally, the triptych is closed and all beings are caught within its frames, but aided by the powers of sorcery the wings can be pushed ajar and the gaps used as pathways between the worlds. Some speculate that the corruption amassing in the world makes the triptych tremble and occasionally open up, making it possible for undead and abominations to enter where gaps occur.

According to the teachings of Katrandama, mystical rituals can also be understood in light of the three worlds. From the physical world comes the building blocks of both flaming servants and the undead raised by Necromancers, but it also requires control over the Spirit World – the grey, barren land of ashes and lost spirits that borders Eternity, where no one alive may travel. Only spirits can enter the infinite void, after which not even they may return. The restless spirits and ghosts that spiritualists speak to and necromancers bend to their will travel the Spirit World. It takes the power of a god to send spirits back from the Eternity beyond the Spirit World's borderland, just as Prios sends Patron Saints to his most loyal servants.

The Yonderworld is thought to be a mist-shrouded wasteland, possible to mistake for the Spirit World, yet vastly different: its nature is corruption. Its fauna consists of abominations, from small Blight Spawns to ancient Blight Beasts of immense power. As stated by Katrandama, the Yonderworld is the world from which humankind fled to this one – an idea that very few mystics are prepared to accept and the Curia has deemed to be contentious and heretical; the humans came over the eastern sea from another continent, fleeing from idol worshippers and sun haters – at least according to the official stands of the Sun Church.

TROLL SINGER

"My voice echoes with the harmony of creation."

Singing as a source of power has its most evident expression in the troll singing skalds, whose voices lay mysteries bare and win battles. Poetry and singing exist in all cultures, but they are most powerful among elves, dwarves and trolls – with the possible addition of ogres. In all of these diverse cultures, singing is often combined with physical attributes – most skalds are true warrior poets that lead their allies to victory using the great power of their voice and muscles.

- **Important Attributes:** *Persuasive 13+, Strong 11+*
- **Suggested Race:** Dwarf, Elf, Ogre, Troll
- **Appropriate Abilities:** *Leader, Mystical Power (usually Combat Hymn), Troll Singing*
- **Suggested Boons:** *Archivist, Commanding Voice, Contacts, Heirloom, Musician, Storyteller*
- **Suggested Burdens:** *Dark Secret, Mystical Mark*

The History of Demonology

Many demonologists regard their trade as vastly different from that of other sorcerers. In essence, they see themselves as explorers, seekers of the truth, and as more advanced compared to mossy wizards who are satisfied poking around in the soil of the "Here-and-Now." Sadly, they will likely never gain the admiration and respect they think they deserve.

According to many legends, the demonologists of the past invited corruption into the world, precisely because they were scratching and tearing at the world's fabric. Later stories blame them for having destroyed the once so lush realm of the Dark Lords, Lyastra. If anything, the demonologists will always be seen as the worst kind of sorcerers.

SPIRITUALIST (PROFESSION) – THE WHITE PATH OF WITCHES

"The dead know and tell those who dare listen."

Witches who solely walk the path of Spiritualists are uncommon and often marked by their journeys through the nothingness, where cold winds blow and the dead wail.

They are often pale of both skin and shadow, cold to the touch and hollow-eyed with a gaze that can pierce shadows and souls. Since contact with the dead is debilitating and dangerous, Spiritualists are respected and sometimes feared even by other witches; their Death Divinations are as remarkable as the wisdom they glean from the Spirit World.

- **Required Abilities:** *Mystical Power (Inherit Wound), Ritualist (Necromancy), Witchcraft, Witchsight*
- **Gifts of the Path:** *Death Divination, Terrify (monstrous trait), Tormenting Spirits*
- **Suggested Boons:** *Augur, Bushcraft, Contacts, Horrifying, Medium, Tough*
- **Suggested Burdens:** *Epileptic, Nightmares*

BLOOD WADER (PROFESSION) – THE RED PATH OF WITCHES

"All witchcraft starts with blood."

Witches who are at one with the blood coursing through their veins sometimes choose the path of the Blood Wader.

They wade where the blood runs thick and passionate and are often marked by their life choices; Blood Waders tend to be impetuous and driven by lust, and their physical transformations often include bestial features in the form of fangs, jakaar-eyes and fur-like hair-growth.

- **Required Abilities:** *Natural Warrior, Medicus, Mystical Power (Shapeshift), Witchcraft*
- **Gifts of the Path:** *Beast Companion, Natural Weapon (monstrous trait), Regeneration (monstrous trait)*
- **Suggested Boons:** *Beast Tongue, Bushcraft, Contacts, Dark Blood, Horrifying, Pet*
- **Suggested Burdens:** *Bestial, Bloodthirst*

DEMONOLOGIST (PROFESSION) – SORCERY DOMAIN

"Daemons? We are the only daemons here."

Beyond the world – or between worlds, if one believes in the existence of multiple worlds – lays the Yonderworld. In the Yonderworld soul-eating creatures roam, indistinguishable from abominations to the common man. Sorcerers appreciate the likeness, but call them *"daemons"* in acknowledgement of their differing origins.

The daemons can be forced, lured or invited into the physical world by those who know of passages between the worlds. These passages may also be used by demonologists to temporarily flee the world – or for casting enemies out of the world, where they might end up face to face with a soul-eating daemon.

- **Required Abilities:** *Mystical Power (Unholy Aura), Ritualist (Desecrating Rite), Sorcery, Witchsight or Loremaster*
- **Gifts of the Specialization:** *Exorcize, Servant Daemon, Summon Daemon, Teleport*
- **Suggested Boons:** *Archivist, Con Artist, Contacts, False Identity, Hideouts*
- **Suggested Burdens:** *Nightmares, Wanted*

GREEN WEAVER (PROFESSION) - THE GREEN PATH OF WITCHES
"My power is rooted in the deep."

The green path winds through Davokar's murky woods, overgrown with shrubbery and roots, visible only to the witches walking it. Where others get stuck on thorn bushes or in mires, the Green Weavers move about with ease, guided by the winds whispering through the leaves and the creaking voices of gnarled tree trunks.

- **Required Abilities:** *Alchemy, Mystical Power (Entangling Vines), Ritualist (Quick Growth), Witchcraft*
- **Gifts of the Path:** *Thorn Cloak, Living Fortress*
- **Suggested Boons:** *Bushcraft, Contacts, Forbidden Knowledge, Green Thumb, Pathfinder, Poison Resilient*
- **Suggested Burdens:** *Dark Secret, Slow*

ILLUSIONIST (PROFESSION) – SCHOOL OF WIZARDRY
"The lie is my truth."

The wizards who specialize in twisting perception journey to the depths of the mind's maze and return wiser and more powerful – provided that they do not get lost in the mirages and dreamworlds; a factual danger for those exploring the possible and imaginable, rather than the real. On the other hand, some illusionists claim that their most unworldly colleagues are those with the greatest understanding of reality; that everything is a lie and that we are free to define what is really true.

Aside from this strong solipsistic tendency there are illusionists who are very enlightened, firmly rooted in a cynical view of the world and the delusions of man, ready to utilize their abilities to the utmost while striving for their goals.

- **Required Abilities:** *Loremaster, Mystical Power (Illusory Correction or Unnoticeable), Ritualist (False Terrain, Illusion), Wizardry*
- **Gifts of the School:** *Bewitching Landscape, Fata morgana, Mirroring*
- **Suggested Boons:** *Contacts, Double-tongue, False Identity, Mirage, Shadow Spawn*
- **Suggested Burdens:** *Addiction, Epileptic*

INQUISITOR (PROFESSION) - ROAD WITHIN THEURGY
"Burn them all and let Prios sort out His own."

For some theurgs, whether among priests or Black Cloaks, the hatred of the dark is so strong that they choose the inquisitor's road: to seek out and destroy the enemies of Prios. Inquisitors are happy to cooperate with templars and other members of the church; they are not interested in understanding the darkness and tend to rely on cunning, ambushes and assassination to reach their goals, never brute force like the templars.

To most inquisitors, sorcerers and their followers have no right to exist, and for that reason no moral consideration is necessary when they are fighting the dark.

- **Required Abilities:** *Mystical Power (Anathema or Unnoticeable), Ritualist (Holy Smoke), Theurgy, Witchsight or Backstab*
- **Gifts of the Road:** *Piercing Gaze, Purgatory*
- **Suggested Boons:** *Archivist, Bloodhound, Contacts, Horrifying, Privileged, Servant*
- **Suggested Burdens:** *Code of Honor, Nightmares*

MENTALIST (PROFESSION)
– SCHOOL OF WIZARDRY
"The will is my law."

Wizards studying the sharp edges and fragile breaking points of the will are often called mindwarpers, or more formally Mentalists. Mindwarpers harden their steel-like wills to be used as both a weapon and armor, thereby proving that the will triumphs over matter.

- **Required Abilities:** *Loremaster, Mystical Power (Bend Will, Mind Throw or Levitate), Ritualist (Clairvoyance or Telepathic Interrogation), Wizardry*
- **Gifts of the School:** *Psychic Thrust, Spell Tunnel*
- **Suggested Boons:** *Archivist, Commanding Voice, Contacts, Manipulator, Privileged, Servant*
- **Suggested Burdens:** *Addiction, Epileptic*

NECROMANCER (PROFESSION)
– SORCERY DOMAIN
"Death is but the beginning."

The Spirit World is the outer realm of the world, where the dead journey towards their final rest – if they are not disturbed by a necromancer on the way.

Necromancers can force the spirits of the outer realm to return, in order to relay their secrets or to occupy a dead body and serve the death mage as a dragoul or some other undead being. An understanding of the mechanics of death also gives the necromancer access to ghastly powers and rituals.

- **Required Abilities:** *Medicus, Mystical Power (Revenant Strike), Ritualist (Raise Undead), Sorcery*
- **Gifts of the Specialization:** *Death Lord, Spirit Walk, Tormenting Spirits*
- **Suggested Boons:** *Archivist, Con Artist, Contacts, False Identity, Forbidden Knowledge, Medium*
- **Suggested Burdens:** *Sickly, Wanted*

PYROMANCER (PROFESSION)
– SCHOOL OF WIZARDRY
"You're about to light a fire you cannot extinguish."

For Pyromancers, the element of fire has a special allure. By studying the essence of fire, the Pyromancer learns to master the exothermic principle to such a degree that fire is transformed into an ally and a shelter, rather than being a dangerous element.

- **Required Abilities:** *Loremaster, Mystical Power (Flame Wall or Brimstone Cascade), Wizardry, Ritualist (Tale of Ashes or Flaming Servant)*
- **Gifts of the School:** *Fire Soul, Twin Servants*
- **Suggested Boons:** *Archivist, Contacts, Fire Forged, Horrifying, Servant*
- **Suggested Burdens:** *Bloodthirst, Impulsive*

CONFESSOR (PROFESSION)
– ROAD WITHIN THEURGY
"In every soul there is strife, mirroring the battle of existence."

Some theurgs regard themselves as herdsmen of the people, as missionaries and healers. These Confessors primarily work to enforce that which is good, keeping the flickering light of Prios alive by providing it with fuel.

They are often found in leading positions, within or outside the church, in order to reach as many people as possible when working to spread light and truth. Many of the highest leaders and greatest theurgs in the church of Prios wander the road of the Confessor.

- **Required Abilities:** *Leader or Medicus, Mystical Power (Holy Aura, Lay on Hands or True Form), Ritualist (Exorcism), Theurgy*
- **Gifts of the Road:** *Atonement, Lifegiver*
- **Suggested Boons:** *Archivist, Augur, Contacts, Privileged, Tough*
- **Suggested Burdens:** *Code of Honor, Dark Secret*

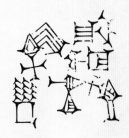

Symbols carved on the ancient stone fundament on which the palace of Mergile is built, likely a curse aimed at the lords and ladies who once lived there.

Ordo Magica's Schools

You could expect that the schools of Ordo Magica operate like guilds or collectives within the organization; that for instance Pyromancers stand together and work to steer the order in a certain direction. But the opposite is often true. The higher up in the hierarchy you climb, the tougher the competition. And it is never more violent than among prominent Mentalists, Illusionists or Pyromancers.

Rogue

THE GREAT WAR seems to be over, or it has at least taken a break. But the power struggle in Ambria continues in the shadows, a struggle that spreads into Davokar. The Queen's Spies, commonly regarded as assassins with a more flattering name, are everywhere. In Yndaros, criminal guilds fight over the city's resources, while a number of gentleman thieves fuel peoples' fantasies about nobles who choose danger over boredom.

Then there are the Sappers, armed with alchemical weapons and skilled in siege techniques that can make the enemy's keep crumble – an art form that also comes in handy when establishing, or attacking, bases and outpost in Davokar. Finally there are the Cult Defectors, who have come to realize that they cannot take part in the deeds ordered by their former leaders. Of course, these defectors are pursued by both witchhunters and the friends they left behind.

What rogues have in common is their versatility and quick counterattacks against those who try to force them in a certain direction or limit their freedom – the latter is captured by the archetypical ability *Rapid Reflexes*.

ROGUES AND THE RACES

Of the races introduced in the *Advanced Player's Guide*, primarily dwarves and the undead are seen as likely rogues. In the case of dwarves, most Ambrians have only met or heard of the families residing in the capital, whose members seems to take pride in behaving like thugs. Regarding the undead, people from all positions and social strata are counted among them, but many of the afflicted tend to lead their wretched lives in the shadows – hoping to avoid becoming the target of some raging mob or a black cloak wanting to study their physiognomy.

ROGUE ABILITIES

The following abilities include those listed in both the *Core Rulebook* and the *Advanced Player's Guide*, sorted according to attributes when relevant.

- **Archetypical ability:** *Rapid Reflexes* (three other abilities from below are required for this ability to be available)
- **Accurate:** *Marksman, Natural Warrior, Polearm Mastery, Steel Throw, Twin Attack*
- **Cunning:** *Alchemy, Beast Lore, Blacksmith,*

Cheap Shot, Loremaster, Medicus, Poisoner, Strangler, Tactician, Trapper
- **Discreet:** *Backstab, Feint*
- **Persuasive:** *Dominate, Leader*
- **Quick:** *Acrobatics, Knife Play, Quick Draw, Rapid Fire*
- **Resolute:** *Steadfast*
- **Strong:** *Steadfast*
- **Vigilant:** *Sixth Sense, Witchsight*
- **General:** *Exceptional Attribute, Equestrian, Opportunist, Recovery, Ritualist*

QUEEN'S SPY (PROFESSION)
"The Queen will find this interesting..."

Already during The Great War there were secret agents working for the King and the court in Alberetor. After the war, the agency lay dormant until the recent troubling times made Queen Korinthia breathe life into what is called the Royal Secretorium.

The Secretorium consists of a number of reliable nobles who secretly enforce the Queen's command to infiltrate various operations and hunt for sensitive information – or spread disinformation. The committee is led by high-borns, while the field work is carried out by nobles of lower rank. A vital part of the operations is aimed at Korinthia's own allies within the Sun Church, Ordo Magica, the military and also the duchies of the realm, meaning the Queen's close relatives. Some spies are not equipped to handle the intrigues and moral ambiguities; others are cast out in the cold after incriminating failures. Former spies of the Queen often live short lives, constantly on the run from both enemies and their former superiors.

- **Important Attributes:** *Cunning 13+, Discreet 11+*
- **Suggested Race:** *Ambrian*
- **Required Abilities:** *Feint, Poisoner or Strangler, Sword Saint, Twin Attack*
- **Other Requirements:** Noble Ambrian (the boon *Privileged*)
- **Unique Ability:** *Pyrotechnics*
- **Suggested Boons:** *Con Artist, Contacts, Enterprise, False Identity, Heirloom, Hideouts, Privileged*
- **Suggested Burdens:** *Arch Enemy, Wanted*

FORMER CULTIST

*"The word of my Master was the law;
now survival is everything."*

Many sorcerers foster cults around themselves and their beliefs, promising drug-induced insights and black salvation to those willing to follow the mystic into the dark. Not many defect from such cults and those who do and survive more than a few days are fewer still, hunted as they are by both the cult they left behind and by witchhunters and black cloaks. The situation is not made any easier by the defector's own burdens – memories of services rendered to please their master and explicitly cruel actions performed in the name of the cult weigh most former cultists down and haunt their nightmares long after leaving the Master.

Some former cultists were once deeply convinced fanatics, while for others the membership was more of a practical choice motivated by ambition or greed. However, if one is to believe the interrogation protocols of the black cloaks, desperation is the most common characteristic among cultists – the injustices of life combined with a charismatic leader who promises redemption and strength can be an attractive combination. But no matter the background, the choices of the cultist were never innocent; the hands of the former cultist are forever colored by blood.

- **Important Attributes:** *Cunning 13+, Resolute 11+*
- **Suggested Race:** *Changeling, Human or Undead*
- **Appropriate Abilities:** *Alchemy, Poisoner, Channeling*
- **Suggested Boons:** *Con Artist, Contacts, Double-tongue, False Identity, Hideouts, Mirage*
- **Suggested Burdens:** *Addiction, Wanted*

GUILD THIEF
"What are you doing on my turf?"

The Guild Thief has a long, if not proud, tradition rooted in Alberetor, a tradition that emerged stronger from the relocation to the north. Each of Ambria's towns have at least one thieves' guild, larger ones often have one based in each district.

Not just anyone is qualified to be a Guild Thief. Sure, pick-pockets and simplistic thugs may prove to be suitable recruits but only the most cunning and agile can hope to gain membership in the guild. To strike unnoticed and know who is untouchable are matters of principle to the Guild Thief.

- **Important Attributes:** *Cunning 13+, Quick 11+*
- **Suggested Race:** Changeling, Human or Goblin
- **Appropriate Abilities:** *Cheap Shot* or *Knife Play, Opportunist, Trapper*
- **Suggested Boons:** *Cat Burglar, Cheat, Con Artist, Contacts, Dexterous, Hideouts*
- **Suggested Burdens:** *Impulsive, Protégé*

GENTLEMAN THIEF (PROFESSION)

"Burglar-proof? We'll see about that..."

Some thieves go one step further than most in terms of flair: to strike without violence and without leaving a trace is not enough for the Gentleman Thieves; they also expect themselves to be able to perform their crimes with finesse. To top things off they often leave some kind of symbol behind – a particular flower, a playing card or a poem composed for the particular victim – to signal who is behind the otherwise inexplicable theft. Some gentleman thieves do not even steal valuables, others steal nothing at all – to them getting into a highly guarded area and leaving their symbol is quite enough.

Gentleman Thieves are among the elite of the thief guilds in Yndaros. Sometimes they are bored nobles who do not need to steal but find it entertaining and thrilling; more often they are of modest breed, longing for a grander life than they can hope to achieve – a life they simultaneously mimic and take revenge on, in their own poetic way.

- **Important Attributes:** *Persuasive 13+, Cunning 11+*
- **Suggested Race:** Changeling, Ambrian
- **Required Abilities:** *Acrobatics, Dominate, Trapper, Sword Saint* or *Twin Attack*
- **Unique Ability:** *Mantle Dance*
- **Suggested Boons:** *Cat Burglar, Contacts, Dexterous, Heirloom, Privileged, Servant*
- **Suggested Burdens:** *Arch Enemy, Code of Honor*

The Thistle of Yndaros

One of Ambria's most notorious Gentleman Thieves goes by the name "The Thistle of Yndaros." He or she is known to move unhindered by guards and security, steals only trivial items as keepsakes and leaves a Twilight Thistle in their stead. The value of the stolen item is always much lower than that of the flower, which has led some to speculate that the Thistle of Yndaros stems from the highest elite, possibly from the royal family. Rilia Kohinoor – the child of Korinthia's dead twin brother Korian, and hence Duke Ynedars sister – is among the suspects, and since she is yet to deny the rumor it flourishes in songs and tales amongst the taverns of Yndaros.

SAPPER

"Your armor and your walls are my combustion chambers."

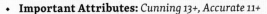

War can be won on battlefields or through sieges, and both of these require advanced field works. In Ambria, most such tasks are handled by Her Majesty's Sapper Corps, 7th Army, Yndarien. Ordo Magica also has a department for battle field alchemy at their headquarters in Agrella; known as The Panzer Alchemists. This elite group of sappers serves the duchy of Kasandrien. The other duchies also have sapper squads, though not of the same caliber. All sappers are trained in the use of siege weapons, from ballistas to trebuchets, and the most qualified can handle alchemical weapons. Sappers are also trained to craft simple fortifications, like barricades for cavaliers, trenches and undermining tunnels.

Ordo Magica has realized that ogres are well equipped to be panzer alchemists and the wizards are supervising attempts to school a number of ogres in the use of alchemical weapons. These pensive giants have also convincingly proven that the heavy alchemical firetube can be employed as an effective, two-handed crushing weapon. This is assumed to increase the life expectancy of the sappers, since those who discharge an alchemical firetube often are at worryingly short distance from the enemy.

- **Important Attributes:** *Cunning 13+, Accurate 11+*
- **Suggested Race:** *Ambrian or Ogre*
- **Appropriate Abilities:** *Alchemy or Blacksmith, Man-at-arms or Two-handed Force, Siege Expert*
- **Suggested Boons:** *Contacts, Dexterous, Enduring March, Forbidden Knowledge, Pack-mule*
- **Suggested Burdens:** *Addiction, Slow*

Races

THERE ARE MANY DIFFERENT cultural beings in the world of *Symbaroum*, and the *Advanced Player's Guide* makes a handful of new races available for character (and NPC) creation. Common to all of them – Elf, Abducted Human, Dwarf, Troll and Undead – is that they have their own special roles to play in the world, and that they for that reason are a bit more challenging to play compared to the races covered by the *Core Rulebook*. Hence, they are better suited for players who already know a thing or two about Ambria and Davokar, and who are looking for a new perspective.

Elf

THE ELVES OF DAVOKAR are not a race per se; instead they are a part of a holy guardian order. Initially, the order involved elves from the virgin regions to the west, where humans have not yet reached and where the Elven civilization is in bloom. This order – by humans known as the Iron Pact – is tasked with preventing the evil that slumbers beneath Davokar's roots and moss from awakening and spreading across the world.

A majority of the elves in Davokar were born into the order. They have never been west and will never go there; to them the Elven lands of old are and remain a dream that will never come true. From when they are young, they are told that their duty lies in Davokar and that they are not welcome in the old lands. The Iron Pact even has a ceremony to initiate young elves into the order, where weeping elders – led by Prince Eneáno – beg newly awakened summer elves for forgiveness for

having forced them to be born, live and die in the Forest of the Death Shadow, Davokar. The life of the pact members is dangerous, their numbers are dwindling and the once so mighty Prince Eneáno is entering his soul's winter – the increasing unpredictability of the Prince has made it possible for other, disagreeing leaders to position themselves for the upcoming power struggle. The dispute concerns the tactics of the battle against the dark – whether it should be fought with arrows and spears or by forging alliances.

The spirited fairies who wake up after their first dormancy enter the phase of the summer elves, and it is they who constitute the backbone of Davokar's guardian force: vigilant hunters armed with spears and bows. Many of them die in battle with abominations or taboo-breakers from the less and less cautious humans in the south. Those who survive eventually reach their second dormancy,

Being an elf does not mean that you know everything about Davokar or the intrigues, factions and history of the Iron Pact. The same goes for representatives of other races. You know what you have experienced; aside from that you must put your faith in tales, legends and rumors – just like the average Ambrian. As a rule of thumb one can say that an elf or a troll knows as much about its place of origin and its people as an Ambrian with the ability Loremaster knows about elves and trolls – sometimes less, since a learned Ambrian probably has access to sources of information which young elves and trolls are not aware of.

a time of tearful grief for the elves. The members of Davokar's Iron Pact all live with the bitter truth that few elves will ever awaken from their second slumber; most wither away before reaching the next life phase.

Perhaps it is for this reason that the holds and forest castles of the Iron Pact always echo with sorrowful songs, lamenting the fallen and withered. Davokar's elves grow fewer and fewer; not even the ever increasing number of abductions can fill the gaps in their ranks. There is, however, a faint light in the gloom: more and more humans are willingly seeking to join the Iron Pact, and the elves working for alliances point out that there are even Ambrians among them.

ELVISH TRAITS, BOONS AND BURDENS

Elvish characters are all *Long-lived*. They also have the trait/burden *Pariah*, since elves are resented by most humans; Ambrians detest them and even barbarians are afraid of them. Also, many elves have the trait *Wisdom of the Ages*, which is acquired like an ability.

If an elf so wishes, he or she can try to impersonate a changeling, usually by changing into cloths made by humans and trying to mimic human manners. A person with the ability *Loremaster* at adept level can see through such a disguise with a passed *Cunning* test; an elf who is recognized as such among humans suffers the negative effects of the trait/burden *Pariah*.

ELVISH NAMES

Spring and summer elves are all given double-names that follow them through the first dormancy; names mirroring their character and/or hopes for what they will be like in their prime. Most who wake up after their second dormancy choose to remove part of the name or change it altogether, but not all. This is up to the individual to decide, and is clearly more a question of taste and style than of function or meaning.

Elven names often have more vowels than consonants and the letter "X" is as uncommon as a name having two consonants in a row.

- **Male Elven Names:** Alal-Roak, Dorael-Ri, Eloan-Eo, Elori, Godrai, Mearoel, Saran-Ri, Tel-Keriel, Kil-Ano
- **Female Elven Names:** Ahara-Vei, Eleanea, Leiána, Gaina-Anali, Keri-Las, Mael-Melian, Naelial, Tara-Kel, Teara-Téana

ELVES AS ADVENTURERS

As a suggestion, player characters of Elven origin should be summer elves, in the second phase of the Elven life-cycle. Sure, it is possible to play older elves, but autumn elves would fare better in a campaign where the other characters are also very powerful since these Elvish beings tend to overshadow most humans in terms of skill, power and insights regarding the deep mysteries of the world.

In any case, elves are uncommon in human settlements and need very strong reasons to travel to such places.

Mediator: The elf has been sent to establish relations with a group of humans and try to teach them about the value of the forest and the dangers of exploration. The mission can be self-imposed but is more likely based on the orders of some superior autumn elf.

Scout: The elf is sent to gather knowledge, to assess the enemy's strengths and weaknesses before the battle that is sure to come. The mission-giver is probably a superior and older elf, either a diplomat or a warmonger.

Exile: Elves who act against the rules of the collective are very uncommon, but are not unheard of in corrupted Davokar. Maybe the player character is one of these? Alternately, the exile is self-imposed, as a result of the elf feeling as if he or she has been disloyal or dishonorable, therefore choosing solitude for a while. Or forever.

Avenger: Elves tend to live, hunt and fight in small groups with strong internal ties. Maybe the others died as a result of treachery by some supposed ally, and the player character survived, by chance or after having managed to escape or beat down the villain's henchmen? As the lone survivor the character feels guilty and will not return home before the traitor has paid for his or her crime.

Abducted Human

IT IS BELIEVED that the elves of Davokar have always abducted human children and left changelings in their stead. Children taken by the elves are called Abductees, and the reasons for them being taken have varied. Initially it was to learn more about and better understand humans; later the motive changed to wanting to foster ambassadors who understood the elves and could live among the barbarians and teach them elven wisdom.

Nowadays (in the Elven sense, meaning the last century), there has been an increasing need for warriors within the Iron Pact – to replace elves fallen in battle, and to offset the growing number of elves that do not survive their first dormancy – the darkening of Davokar causes fewer and fewer elves to wake to their summer phase. Hence, it is not uncommon to see abducted humans hunt and fight alongside summer elves in the warbands of the Pact.

The elves have long since known that abductees are loyal and good learners, but much to their surprise some of them have also proven capable of wisdom. Very few elves would ever admit this; to most elves the abducted humans are almost akin to faithful pets, useful and absolutely possible to love, but never to be regarded as equals.

ABDUCTED HUMAN TRAITS, BOONS AND BURDENS

Abducted Humans have the trait *Bushcraft*. The abductees speak Elvish but cannot read Elven writing if they have not learned the ability *Loremaster*.

ABDUCTED HUMAN NAMES

The abductees are named by their foster parents, often in a way that sounds human to the elves and seldom with names consisting of more than two syllables. They should be easy to pronounce and remember, preferably also easy to roar if the need arises. Aside from that, the names often have more consonants than vowels and almost never two consonants in a row, just like Elven names.

- **Male Abductee Names:**
  Awan, Beo, Eral, Gaer, Kael, Lo, Mael, Orel, Tham, Tir

- **Female Abductee Names:** Anga, Beha, Erli, Fera, Inda, Lonam, Una, Undi, Vird

ABDUCTEES AS ADVENTURERS

Abducted Humans tend to leave the Iron Pact for the same reasons elves sometimes do – as mediators, scouts, exiled or avengers – but may also have a much more personal reason for becoming an adventurer:

Runaway: For some reason – curiosity, home-sickness, abuse – the abductee chooses to flee to the realm of humans, to become a special sort of stranger.

Dwarf

THE SHORT AND WIRY people humans call dwarves have a history shrouded in mystery. Looking at the dwarves settled in Yndaros, they display no interest in the history of their kind; they are a people on the move, aimed towards the future, fleeing a dark past that has given them a sense of community, but without peace or meaning. The dwarven perspective is rooted in the sanctity of the family, the secrets of the spoken word and the conviction that the world is their common enemy. Gamalga of Kadizar, a sage interested in dwarves, is said to have stated that: *"The family is their shield, the language their weapon and the world their battlefield".*

Gamalga also spoke of the origin of the dwarves. After many fruitless conversations with the dwarves in Yndaros and at the fortress Küam Zamok, Gamalga realized that she would get better answers from elves and trolls, and that these claimed to have never met dwarves before the fall of Symbaroum. They were most likely created in the old empire and Gamalga summarizes her meager findings as follows:

"They emerged as worms in the rotting carcass of the World Serpent and were given wit by Symbaroum's sorcerers, to make them better slaves. However, the birth of the people forever bound them to the world and its fate, and because of this bond they early on developed a forceful counterculture which still marks them. The ancestral mothers and fathers of the dwarves created a language with hidden codes and secret double-meanings, so intricate that not even the masters could understand. The dwarves never wrote anything down, since texts could be read, interpreted and even decoded by the lords of Symbaroum. The dwarves kept their dreams to themselves and their voices echoed with the fate of the world.

Both elves and trolls confirm that there is power inherent in some dwarven speech, and imply that those who made the dwarves, Symbaroum's princes, in time learned to hate their creations and fear the power of their very language. After the fall of Symbaroum, the chronicle of the dwarven race describes an arduous journey in the shadow of death, continuously attacked and hunted by others. Nowadays, the descendants of the few who survived Symbaroum's ruin have spread to many places and their fates are seemingly very different. Apparently, the families in Yndaros are members of a once ruling elite in Küam Zamok, cast out after a bloody revolution – hence, the organized villains encountered in Ambria's capital are in fact dwarven nobles, used to ruling and giving orders, but incapable of creating even the most essential items themselves. More dubious scraps of information say that their inability to get along has to do with the order of succession in the realm they left behind, and the right to a throne which none of them will ever conquer."

The people of Ambria have formed their opinions based on the dwarves in Yndaros, and they are not a very welcoming sort. They demand nothing of others, other than being allowed to mind their own business. To dwarves, the will of the family – as interpreted by the elders – is superior to the will of the individual, meaning that they often appear to have two sets of moral standards: one strictly coded and aimed at the family; another aimed at outsiders and often described as *"a lack of morality"* by their neighbors – since actions which only affect outsiders have no bearing on the internal family relations.

The speech of the Yndarian dwarves is still today so intricate and filled with codes, double-meanings and obscure idioms that their everyday conversations are close to unintelligible to bystanders, no matter how learned. It is also true that their voices have a particular power that some individuals know to make use of. Furthermore, their memory-techniques are highly developed, making it possible for them to run complex "businesses" in Yndaros without writing down a single number or word.

DWARVEN TRAITS, BOONS AND BURDENS

All characters of the dwarven kind have the trait *Earth Bound*, the boon *Absolute Memory* and the burden *Pariah*. Many dwarves also have the mystical power *Retribution*, but functioning as a normal ability. For dwarves, this particular power gives no corruption, not when it is acquired, not when it is used – this only applies to this power and this race.

DWARVEN NAMES

Judging by the dwarves living in Yndaros, they have a fondness for names which contain many hard consonants, such as k, t and r. Aside from that, there seems to be no difference between male and female names: they are inherited within the family and between generations without concern for gender. All dwarves have also family surnames, just like the Ambrian nobles. However, it appears as if younger dwarves must earn the right to call themselves by their family name, preferably by impressing their relatives and making them proud.

- **Dwarf Names:** Artek, Bolkor, Brana, Dobril, Dranek, Dusa, Jarok, Lazek, Margor, Mirek, Radmil, Stana, Vesnek, Vlador, Yaruk

DWARVES AS ADVENTURERS

Dwarves who choose or are forced to leave their families in Yndaros are lonely and often dangerous individuals. However, for some dwarves, the seclusion becomes the start of the search for a new family, defined by other characteristics than blood. The following reasons may explain why the dwarven player character has left Yndaros to head out into the world.

Dreams of Doom: The dwarf is haunted by nightmares of doom and death, for its family or the world as a whole. He or she has left the community to become a seeker, hoping to determine the meaning of the dreams and, ideally, learn how to avert the disaster and protect all loved-ones.

Life-debt: An outsider has saved the life of the dwarf without asking for anything in return. The character wants to get free from this debt by serving the outsider and doing whatever he or she says. For a dwarf, this is an acceptable reason for being away from the family.

Outcast: The dwarf has behaved disloyally, maybe challenged the head of the family or questioned the family's position in the order of succession. For this, he or she is banished, temporarily or permanently. To most dwarves, exile is a punishment worse than death.

Spy: The dwarf is not exiled but pretends to be, with the intent of gaining access to secrets that the family needs. Alternately, the player character may be sent to perform some illegal deed, for instance hunting down a fugitive with a stronger claim to the dwarven crown than the character's family.

Dwarf Law

If an action against an outsider does not affect the family, it has no consequence, no matter how cowardly or cruel it may appear to others. Among the people of Yndaros this is known as "Dwarf Law"; what a dwarf can get away with, he or she will likely do.

Dwarven Families in Yndaros

The most prominent dwarven families in Yndaros are named Valotzar, Alzerek and Baldysik, of which the first seems to have adapted best to the new conditions of life. Other known families – among which most are (permanently or at times) allied to the ones mentioned earlier – include Kalatra, Maretko, Obrutz, Skruztsa, Statzak, Vanoviz and Urbanik. Then there is the Merotzak family in Thistle Hold, though it is unclear if they are of the dwarven royal blood-line or not…

Troll

TO ALL AMBRIANS and most barbarians, the word troll is synonymous with bloody death. Some witches and Ambrian scholars know better and claim that there is much truth hidden in the barbarian legends about troll kingdoms below ground, where the trolls holds court and mighty hymns are sung in halls adorned with beautiful things crafted by Trollish hands. However, those who say that trolls can be civilized also admit that individuals encountered on the surface are dangerous: if a troll leaves the Abyss, it often has a bloody reason to do so.

Trolls do not reproduce, that is for the goblins to do. When goblins feel death breathing down their necks, they ventures down into the Underworld. There they finally fall down and a cocoon-like tissue sprouts out of their bodies until it covers them completely. Many die while slumbering, but the few who survive develop into the beastly creatures that Ambrians call Rage Trolls. Some of these are found by other trolls while still in the hibernation phase, and are brought to an underground realm for care and safety. The majority crawl upwards to the surface, naked and famished, ready to feed on anything crossing their paths. Some of these crude creatures are found by surface-living Liege Trolls – lords who either dress them in clothes and cultivate their nature, or whip them into obedience and make them the front-runners in their robber bands.

The troll civilization differs a lot from human societies. The value and worth of a troll is determined by what he or she can bring to the community, whether in the form of a warrior's protection, a craftsman's items or a skald's songs. The most ruthless and vigorous trolls manage to secure a place among the leaders and become members of the Rulers Caste – a place they only keep so long as they can defend it through fighting and scheming. The trolls often challenge each other to contests as a part of the social game. In most cases, the contest is physical, but it can just as well be about who can keep singing longest or who can craft the most powerful artifact. Physical fights are by far most frequent and even though these confrontations are ritualized they sometimes end in death, if only by accident.

Trolls, Goblins and Ogres

Trolls, Goblins and Ogres have a common origin, which is known to all trolls.

With increasing age, all goblins feel drawn to the lonely depths of Davokar. It is there they die, alone on the road towards the Underworld – if they do not die from illness or violence before then. The dying goblins seek out a secluded spot where they undergo a re-markable transformation; they pupate. Most of them die in the cocoon, but for some the pupation is nothing more than a new step in their life-cycle, since they develop into trolls while safely slumbering inside the cocoon.

At times, something goes wrong as the goblin matures in its cocoon and the progeny – who, without claws, has to scratch its way to freedom – looks very much like a troll but is without some of the defining features. Among Ambrians and barbarians such creatures are called ogres. These "misshapen trolls" also lack the rage trolls' hunger and strong instinct to head down into the Underworld. Instead, the ogres often leave the depth of the woods and cling to the first person they happen to encounter.

A worrying tendency is that more and more ogres seem to be born, something the trollsingers claim has to do with Davokar growing darker. In general, trolls regard ogres with mixed emotions, but for most they are seen as a kind of distant cousins who deserve their help or at least their compassion.

Education through physical and spiritual challenges is deeply rooted within their culture and all trolls aim to grow stronger, both as individuals and as a group. Duels are regarded as the only viable method for achieving this hardening of body and collective. An often heard idiom which captures this says: *"If I break you, our people grow weaker; if I let you get off lightly, you grow weaker."*

Chapter Master Argoi at the Kurun-chapter has described this in the following way: *"The physical and moral life-style of trolls is clearly demonstrated in the encounter with other folks, since such encounters provide no incentives for showing mercy. In fact, this brutal killer-culture grows even crueler if the enemy surrenders or demonstrates any kind of weakness, because such behavior evokes a special kind of loathing. After all, an enemy who acts courageously is worthy of respect and may therefore be spared, according to troll logic."*

TROLLS' TRAITS, BOONS AND BURDENS

Player characters who are trolls can acquire the monstrous traits *Armored*, *Natural Weapon*, *Regeneration* and *Robust* as if they were abilities. Trolls are also *Long-lived* and have the burden *Pariah*, since they scare humans to death.

Trolls may try to impersonate ogres, usually by cutting off their horns, wearing human clothes and adopting the often leisurely movement pattern of the ogres. A person who has at least adept level in *Loremaster* can see through such a disguise by passing a *Cunning* test. Also, while ogres have the burden *Pariah*, most humans have learned that ogres are usually harmless. On the other hand, a troll who is recognized as such will have grave problems, as most humans tend to react by calling for the Town Guard and troll-slaying heroes.

TROLL NAMES

Just like dwarves, trolls make no difference between men and women when it comes to names; a troll gets the name he or she deserves. Also, they usually rename themselves several times during their lifespan, depending on what they experience. It should be noted that the names differ with age, or possibly between more or less powerful trolls. This is most clearly indicated by the use of the letter X, which usually can be found in the names of mightier individuals.

- **Names of young trolls:** Aka, Aroha, Erula, Hibne, Ogmaka, Raham, Riomata, Skadal, Verhar
- **Names of old/powerful trolls:** Aravarx, Etaxa, Noxar, Ognyx, Rirbax, Vouax, Uhux

TROLLS AS ADVENTURERS

By tradition, trolls are tightly bound to their societies and need more than common curiosity to head out into the world. Here follows a couple of examples or incentives which can drive a troll character to adventure beyond the domains of its kin:

Artifact-collector: The crafting-skills of trolls are held in high esteem even among elves, and many troll-made artifacts have been given as gifts to allies – or been stolen by enemies. Trolls feel closely connected to everything crafted by their kind and it is important to them that such objects not remain in the wrong place or in the wrong hands. The character is sent to collect one or more of these lost treasures, either from ancient tombs, Symbarian ruins or from unworthy, soon-to-be-dead thieves.

Educational Journey: Trolls usually send their young ones abroad to learn about the world and its creatures. The destination may vary, but the goal is always to come to terms with the powers which shape the world. Before, many traveled to the closest Iron Pact settlement, but nowadays humankind and above all the newly arrived Ambrians are as interesting, or more interesting, than the elves.

Undead

SOMETHING IS NOT RIGHT with the world. The shadows grow darker as the corruption grows deeper, and natural laws are failing in this twilight of existence. One clear piece of evidence of this downfall is the increasing number of undead.

Undead, as in thoroughly corrupted creatures thirsting for the life-force of the living, are nothing new: the Dark Lords confronted during The Great War awoke whole armies of these gravely cold beings, and Davokar's ancient tombs harbor their fair share of vengeful undead.

However, a new kind of undead creatures has recently appeared in Ambria. People who die – or should have died – rise again. The Black Cloaks, who secretly are investigating the worrying rumors, seem to think that Ambria's capital is at the heart of this horrific development. Reports sent to the monastery in the Titans include a slain cultist in Yndaros who clawed himself from his grave and disappeared into the night, a man dead from old age who awakened as if having slumbered and was chased away after having gone to his work-place, and a woman of noble birth who died in childbirth and later escaped the family crypt to kidnap her living child. All these three were later tracked and found, one of them killed by a group of templars, one captured by Black Cloaks for study-purposes and the third caught by an angry mob but lucky enough to escape being burned at the stake – all of them telling examples of what the undead will face if revealed for what they are.

Common for all these new undead beings is that they show clear indications of actually being dead – they are cold, they do not bleed or eat or sleep – yet their minds appear to be intact. And they are all very slowly decaying towards their final death, which might come centuries after their first death.

UNDEAD TRAITS, BOONS AND BURDENS

Undead player characters are thoroughly corrupt from the start. Like others of his or her kind, the undead character has a mind and free will; they are not howling abominations bent on destruction.

In other respects, this kind of person is very different from other characters. He or she does not sleep, cannot eat normal food and does not breath – besides as a force of habit and to be able to talk. They can drink in small doses and often do so to blend in among the living. Another important difference is that the undead do not heal: they have to consume fresh, raw flesh or drink blood to regain *Toughness* (see the trait *Undead*, level I).

The social consequences of being undead are profound; the undead must constantly struggle to avoid being discovered, and should they fail they will be hounded by witchhunters and Black Cloaks. An undead character must pass a *[Discreet←Vigilant]* test in situations where they interact with living beings. If the character uses the elixir Twilight Tincture, no test is needed. However, this does not stop creatures with *Witchsight* from having a chance to expose the undead with a passed *[Vigilant←Discreet]* test. In that case, the ritual *Exchange Shadow* can be of use.

All undead player characters start with the trait *Undead* (I), and can purchase higher levels as if it was an ability. The character is also allowed to acquire the monstrous traits *Gravely Cold* and *Terrify* as if they were abilities, but having them from the start is optional.

The undead are thoroughly described on page 196 in the *Core Rulebook*. Players of the undead must read that section, and their Game Masters must consider what effects playing an undead character will have on the game.

Traits

THIS VERY SHORT CHAPTER describes two new traits, mirroring the collective wisdom of the elves along with the dwarves' tie to the roots and fate of the world.

WISDOM OF THE AGES

Through the eons, the elves have amassed a vast collective wisdom; a deep well of knowledge and insights which many elves can access through meditation. The character is one of those who may use the know-how of previous generations to solve problems at hand.

It is not without risks; in the twilight of the world, the process spawns corruption. *Wisdom of the Ages* gives temporary corruption as if it was a mystical power.

Novice	**Full turn.** The character gets lost in a short trance. With a passed *Resolute* test, it gains access to the novice level of an optional ability, *Mystical Traditions*, *Ritualist* and *Mystical Power* excluded. Only one ability at a time can be accessed in this way; changing to another one requires a new trance. The ability can be used for the rest of the scene, before fading from memory.
Adept	**Active.** As I, but the closer connection to the collective memory makes the trance even shorter.
Master	**Active.** As II, but the individual can dig deeper into the collective memory. With a passed *Resolute* test, it gains access to the adept level of an optional ability.

EARTH BOUND

The creature is bound to the world in an intimate way, as if originating from the bones of the world and still being part of its foundation.

It has no soul and suffers damage instead of corruption; temporary corruption causes bleeding wounds on its body.

Permanent corruption instead causes a permanent reduction to the basis for calculating the creatures *Pain Threshold*. In practice, this means that the *Pain Threshold* is reduced by 1 for every other point the creature suffers in permanent corruption. Its *Toughness* is not affected. If the *Pain Threshold* is reduced to zero, the creature dies of internal bleeding and failing organs.

Once dead, the creature cannot become undead and it cannot be contacted with the ritual *Necromancy*. The corpse decays and reunites with the slop and dust of creation, without leaving any kind of spiritual trace behind.

One of the stairs up to the plateau surrounding Serand's Pyramid – the enormous ruin a few days ride north of Karvosti. Dozens, maybe hundreds, of expeditions have been there over the years; still new finds are often reported from its depths.

Boons and Burdens

BOONS AND BURDENS have their primary use in social challenges and in problem-solving; they add color to and set the character apart from others without having the same impact on combat situations as traits and abilities do. Basically, boons and burdens function very much like the single-level traits featured in the *Core Rulebook*, so with the book in your hand, traits like *Contacts* and *Bushcraft* are regarded as boons, while *Pariah* is considered a burden.

THE RULES FOR BOONS and burdens are optional and each gaming group must decide whether it adds something positive to the game or not. If put into play, these rules will primarily affect the way characters are created and developed.

Boons can be bought for 5 *Experience* each. Hence, a novice level ability – worth 10 *Experience* – may be switched for two boons when the player character is created. Burdens will instead add 5 extra *Experience*, to be used for acquiring one boon or saved for the future (or for re-rolls, if the optional rule Re-roll for Experience is used). Another option is to choose two burdens and trade them for a novice level ability. It is recommended that a character does not have more than two to three boons and one or two burdens – after that, the character quickly becomes more difficult, rather than more fun, to play.

Boons

BOONS ARE SKILLS or resources which are effective for handling social challenges and problem-solving situations, instead of being useful in combat. Anyone can acquire a boon, it is most often a question of practice. However, since the various boons occur naturally in different environments, they are still chiefly relevant for the members of certain occupations and archetypes, at least at the start. It should also be added that the boons listed in this section are great for adding color to the character, for a lower cost in *Experience* than abilities.

Some of the boons may be purchased multiple times, meaning that its bonus can be from +1 to +3. These are marked with a * in the list on page 52, and it is also mentioned in the description of the boons in question.

ABSOLUTE MEMORY

The character stems from a culture that by tradition does not use writing, but which instead has developed memory techniques to preserve and transmit vital knowledge. He or she remembers everything seen or heard, which means that the player may ask the Game Master about details perceived by the player character during its past adventures. The Game Master must answer as thoroughly as possible.

ARCHIVIST

The character is trained to organize and search for information. He or she gains a +1 bonus when researching in archives and libraries.

Archivist can be acquired multiple times, up to a maximum bonus of +3 on relevant tests.

AUGUR

The character has always seen signs others have missed, and has a +1 bonus on tests for rituals dealing with fate or hidden information: *Fortune-telling*, *Holy Smoke* and *Oracle*.

Augur can be acquired multiple times, up to a maximum bonus of +3 on relevant tests.

BEAST TONGUE

The character can speak to creatures from the monster category Beasts. Beasts have their limitations but can answer questions about which creatures are in, or have traveled through, an area, and also estimate their numbers (one, two or many). The beasts do not perform any services; they talk to the character as if they were equals.

BLOODHOUND

The player character has a developed sense for finding people, no matter if the traces of their presence are found on the ground, in a lair or among discovered belongings. The character has a +1 bonus on *Vigilant* and *Cunning* tests to find and follow tracks, or to figure out where someone is hiding.

Bloodhound can be acquired multiple times, up to a maximum bonus of +3 on relevant tests.

BLOOD TIES

The character has established a mystical blood tie to a creature of a different race. Because of this link, he or she can choose to invest *Experience* in order to acquire a trait belonging to the race of the blood-friend. It is most likely that the Blood Tie of the character is linked to another Cultural Being, but beasts and other creatures are a possibility. The story of how the character came to enter into the relationship is probably interesting

and telling of his or her life history, maybe also of the character's morals and worldviews.

CARTOGRAPHER

The character has been trained to draw precise maps – a sought-after skill in this age of exploration. He or she gets a +1 bonus on tests regarding orientation and location, both on the surface and down in the Underworld.

Cartographer can be acquired multiple times, up to a maximum bonus of +3 on relevant tests.

CAT BURGLAR

The character is trained to open locks, latches and bolts, and gets a +1 bonus on all tests to pick locks – the test is made against *Quick* if the burglar is in a hurry or against *Discreet* when the challenge is to not alert anyone on the other side of the door. A *Discreet* test is also rolled to conceal that the lock has been picked, should someone investigate later on.

Cat Burglar can be acquired multiple times, up to a maximum bonus of +3 on relevant tests.

CHEAT

The character is trained to cheat in games and knows how to avoid detection. He or she gets a +1 bonus on *Cunning* tests when gambling, and to get away with it the cheat must pass a *[Discreet←Vigilant]* test versus the opponent with the highest *Vigilant*, a test that the cheat gets a second chance to succeed on. *Cheat* can be combined with *Gambler* for additional bonuses.

Cheat can be acquired multiple times, up to a maximum bonus of +3 on relevant tests.

COMMANDING VOICE

The character has a well-tuned and loud voice, able to rise above the clamor of combat. This provides a +1 bonus to *Persuasive* tests in situations when the character gives direct orders to allies.

The boon *Commanding Voice* can be acquired multiple times, up to a maximum bonus of +3 on relevant tests.

CON ARTIST

The character is trained to quickly twist the truth, and to generalize or exaggerate when it is called for. The character has a +1 bonus on *Persuasive* and *Vigilant* tests regarding lies; hence, both for making a lie and noticing when others are lying. The lie's veracity is usually found out quickly, so the liar must hurry if he or she is to take advantage of it.

Con Artist can be acquired multiple times, up to a maximum bonus of +3 on relevant tests.

DARK BLOOD

Dark blood flows through the character's veins, passed down from an ancestor, or as a result of being cursed. Maybe the player character was simply born in the wrong part of Davokar at the wrong time. The dark blood always comes with some form of physical stigma, represented by the burden *Bestial*.

The character may acquire and develop the following monstrous traits as though they were ordinary abilities: *Natural Weapon, Armored, Robust, Regeneration, Wings*.

DEXTEROUS

The character has unusually nimble fingers and gains a +1 bonus on all *Discreet* tests when trying to steal items or hide items he carries.

Dexterous can be acquired multiple times, up to a maximum bonus of +3 on relevant tests.

DOUBLE-TONGUE

Double-tongue is a language developed by the Thieves Guild in Yndaros – you say one thing but mean another. This way, sensitive conversations can be held within earshot of outsiders. If multiple characters know *Double-tongue*, they can speak about secrets without risk – provided that the bystanders do not know the language as well...

ENDURING MARCH

After having marched many, many miles in military columns or through the wilds, the player character does not have to make a test to endure walking at Death March speed. Damage also heals as normal during Forced Marches. The expertise of the character benefits those around him or her, and all traveling companions get a second chance to endure the strain of walking at Death March speed. Furthermore, they may roll a *Strong* test to see if they heal naturally during a Forced March.

ENTERPRISE

The character owns some kind of establishment – a small tavern, a smaller store or some other simple craft service like a cobbler or trinket shop. Other alternatives are a theater or a troop of acrobats. The enterprise can be stationary in a place often visited by the characters between adventures, or it can be mobile in the form of a wagon or a river boat if that feels more reasonable.

Once per adventure (or in-between adventures), the character may roll a *Cunning* (for artisans) or *Persuasive* (for services) test. A success renders a profit of 10+1D10 thaler, after all expenses have been paid. If more than one character has *Enterprise*, it can be parts of the same establishment or business. If so, both characters roll a profit test each.

ESCAPE ARTIST

The character has loose joints and is trained to utilize this in order to get free from bonds or squeeze through narrow passages. He or she can also get free from the clutches of an enemy or out of traps such as nets and snares. In all these cases, the character gets a second chance to pass the test, no matter which attribute is used.

FALSE IDENTITY

The character has a false identity, complete with clothes, equipment and papers to back it up. The identity is so well-crafted that it cannot be exposed unless the person who created it (usually a prominent member of the organization or faction to which the character belongs) discloses it – or if the character does something clearly revealing.

FIRE FORGED

The character was born beneath a glowing celestial phenomenon or was the only one to survive a devastating fire. He or she has a mystical +1 protection against fire and has also a +1 bonus on all success tests related to the use of, or resistance to, fire and flames.

FLEET-FOOTED

The creature or person moves at an unusually high speed. In situations where precision counts, the movement is 13 meters per turn. And in connection to the rule on Flight & Hunt (page 102), the trait gives a +3 *Quick* bonus.

FORBIDDEN KNOWLEDGE

The character has somehow come to possess the secrets of the mystical traditions regarding alchemy and artifact crafting; maybe as a result of espionage or after having served a far-traveled Master. With the abilities *Alchemy* and *Artifact Crafting*, he or she has the capability to create all elixirs and artifacts, including those belonging to the secrets of other traditions.

GAMBLER

The character gets a +1 bonus on all *Cunning* tests when gambling or playing strategy games like Prios' Sun. Also, he or she gets +1 on *Vigilant* to expose cheats. *Gambler* can be combined with *Cheat* for added bonuses.

Gambler can be acquired multiple times, up to a maximum bonus of +3 on relevant tests.

GREEN THUMB

The character has a mystical connection to all growing things and has a +1 bonus on tests related to challenges in the wilds, such as orienting in the woods, finding food and shelter, and detecting/avoiding natural traps. The bonus also applies to all *Alchemy* tests.

Green Thumb can be acquired multiple times, up to a maximum bonus of +3 on relevant tests.

HEIRLOOM

The character has inherited a family heirloom. Choose an optional weapon or armor from the lists in the *Core Rulebook* or the *Advanced Player's Guide*, except items with some kind of mystical quality.

HIDEOUTS

Many organizations and networks regularly establish hideouts in Ambria and the outer regions of Davokar; guilds and factions like witches, the Queen's Rangers and most barbarian clans maintain such places for their members. The character knows of, and has access to, a series of such hideouts, linked to a specific group. There he or she can lay low and replace or acquire vital equipment, including weapons and armor.

When the character needs a hideout, he or she rolls a *Cunning* test – a success means that the character recalls the location of a place in the vicinity. The location is hidden, safe and contains equipment to a value of 10 thaler; the character decides what is kept in the hideout, items and/or coins. He or she who takes something from a hideout is expected to replace it later, or at least report what was taken and for what purpose.

HORRIFYING

The character knows how to be threatening in an effective way and can scare people into acting according to his or her will, if only for a short while. He or she gets a +1 bonus to all *Persuasive* tests pertaining to threats, interrogation and coercion. The effect is momentary; later the victim will likely backbite the character when a chance presents itself.

Horrifying can be acquired multiple times, up to a maximum bonus of +3 on relevant tests.

IMPRESSIONIST

The character is a skilled impressionist, whether trying to impersonate a type of person belonging to his own race or imitating a specific individual. He or she gains a +1 bonus on *Discreet* tests when trying to impersonate others. If the character only aims to act as a type of person (for instance a town

guardsman) rather than a specific individual, he or she also gets a second chance to pass the test.

Impersonating a type of person belonging to another race is harder; the impressionist may try but gets a second chance to fail the test. Specific individuals of another race are impossible to imitate in a credible way.

Impressionist can be acquired multiple times, up to a maximum bonus of +3 on relevant tests.

MANIPULATOR

The character knows how to manipulate others, using flattery, threats, or a combination thereof. He or she gets a +1 bonus to *Persuasive* versus a specific person during the scene. It takes time to influence someone; it requires a scene of emotional manipulations to achieve the intended effect. On the other hand, the influence lasts longer than when simply lying – the victim accepts the sentiments as its own and will defend them long after the manipulator has left the place.

Manipulator can be acquired multiple times, up to a maximum bonus of +3 on relevant tests.

MEDIUM

The character grew up in the presence of ghosts and developed a connection to the reality of spirits. He or she gets a +1 bonus on *Vigilant*, *Resolute* and *Persuasive* tests aimed at noticing, interacting with or subduing restless spirits. The bonus also applies to attempts to resist a spirit's powers, when aimed at the player character.

Medium can be acquired multiple times, up to a maximum bonus of +3 on relevant tests.

MIRAGE

The person has a mystical gift and may weave momentary mirages from thin air; flames that emit no heat jump between his or her hands, tiny figures of light dance in the air, and so on. The character can also weave false images over smaller objects, for instance making pebbles appear as shining coins. Over time, the mirage will not fool anyone as its effect wears off at the end of the scene.

With *Mirage*, the person may roll against *Persuasive* to dupe someone into accepting fake goods or payment in the form of illusory coins, to a maximum "value" of a hundred thaler. Also, *Mirage* grants +1 to *Persuasive* when the player character threatens someone with "powerful magic."

MUSICIAN

The character is a talented musician and possibly trained in the art of singing and playing an instrument. He can give himself or his group of allies a +1 bonus on all *Persuasive* tests; everyone likes to hear a good song. A musician's skills can even save the character's life, as a beautiful voice and the sound of well-tuned strings can calm members of the monster category Beasts – if no one threatens the creature, a *[Persuasive←Resolute]* test will stop it from attacking. The character and its allies may then back away and find another route forward.

Musician can be acquired multiple times, up to a maximum bonus of +3 on relevant tests.

PATHFINDER

The character has well-tuned senses for spotting and following tracks, both below ground and on the surface. He or she gets a second chance to pass all *Vigilant* tests when trying to follow a trail or find the way to, or back from, a place.

PACK-MULE

The character is used to carrying heavy loads. The basis for calculating his or her carrying capacity is *Strong* ×1.5. For information on carrying capacity, see Encumbrance on page 100.

PET

The character has a trusty friend in the form of a jakaar or mare cat - any beast will do, so long as it poses weak resistance. The pet is unswervingly loyal to the player character. In combat and problem-solving it is played by the player as a second character, but it does not gain *Experience* and cannot develop its stats (for that you need the ritual *Familiar*). If the pet dies, the character can have it replaced at the start of the next adventure.

POISON RESILIENT

By carefully exposing himself to toxins, the character has built up a remarkable resilience. Poisons affect the character at one tier lower than normal - a strong poison has the effect of a moderate dose; moderate becomes weak and a weak dose only inflicts 1 point of damage during the turns it is active. The time-frame is not affected, only the amount of damage per turn. Regarding toxins that have other negative effects than damage, the character has instead a second chance on tests to resist them.

SERVANT

The character has a personal servant. It may be an employed attendant, a serf chamber boy or something like that. The servant is loyal to the player character, but is otherwise useless in terms of skills (weak resistance). It can perform simple chores,

stand guard at night or convey messages to others, but it will not contribute in dangerous situations. The servant is played by the Game Master and should be provided a suitable personality.

SHADOW SPAWN

The character was born during a solar eclipse and ever since then shadows are drawn to him or her. The shadow spawn gets a +1 bonus on all *Discreet* tests when sneaking or hiding.

Shadow Spawn can be acquired multiple times, up to a maximum bonus of +3 on relevant tests.

SOULMATE

The character has a soulmate, either in the romantic or in the brotherly sense. Irrespective of which, the character may telepathically communicate simple messages and feelings to the counterpart. They always know approximately where the other person is and if he or she is in any kind of trouble.

The counterpart may be a non-player character important to the game or the character of another player; talk to your gaming friends and decide what is best. In the latter case, it is enough that one of the characters acquires the boon in question.

STORYTELLER

The character is a gifted storyteller and no matter if he narrates legends, religious myths or burlesque tales he will impress the audience. The storyteller gains a +1 bonus on *Persuasive* tests when attempting to weave a credible story to impress listeners, and is skilled enough to earn an income from his performances (see Income from Boons, page 103).

Storyteller can be acquired multiple times, up to a maximum bonus of +3 on relevant tests.

TELLTALE

The character has ears and a tongue for gossip and can sniff out rumors and also pass them on to new places. He or she gets a +1 bonus to all tests in connection to hearing, spreading or realizing the truth behind rumors.

Telltale can be acquired multiple times, up to a maximum bonus of +3 on relevant tests.

TOUGH

The character has a tough body and a strong soul, meaning that his or her heart keeps beating when the hearts of others would give up. A player character with the boon *Tough* may always roll death tests with two dice, and choose to accept the most favorable outcome.

Short- or Long-lived?

The traits *Short-* and *Long-lived* are not to be regarded as boons or burdens, as they primarily have a mood-setting effect – they have no impact on the rules, and there are very few situations in game where the theoretical lifespan of a player character is of significance.

Burdens

BURDENS ARE NEGATIVE traits which add to the character's history and also provide extra *Experience* to spend on abilities/boons. Using burdens is considered an optional rule, so the gaming group has to reach a common understanding on whether or not to do so.

ADDICTION

The character has developed an addiction and must have a dose of his or her drug each day, or suffer from withdrawal symptoms. The drug (wine, dream snuff, daft root or similar) costs one shilling per dose. An alchemist can create the drug for himself or a friend for half that price. Withdrawal symptoms give a –1 modification to all tests and grow worse day-by-day, up to –5. Each day without the drug, the character must also pass a *[Resolute -the abstinence modification]* test. If it fails, he or she will abandon all other projects and start hunting for the daily dose.

ARCH ENEMY

The character has, by actions or name, made an arch enemy. This individual has devoted his or her existence to destroying – and in the end, taking – the character's life. At least once during each adventure, the influence of the arch enemy will show. He or she primarily acts through others; hiring thugs or spreading lies in the hope that others will make life difficult for the character. Exactly who this arch enemy is, why he or she hates the character and what resources are at hand, is for the player and Game Master to decide. However, it cannot be someone who is easily avoided or stopped from acting out his or her hatred.

BESTIAL

The player character has a bestial appearance, in the form of one (or a few) conspicuous traits – jakaar eyes, aboar tusks, lindworm scales on arms and neck, or something else arousing fear and disgust. Concealing the traits requires the character to pass a *[Discreet←Vigilant]* test. If the test is failed, the character will have a second chance at failing all *Persuasive* tests concerning pleas for help or protection. However, the bestial exterior grants a second chance to pass all *Persuasive* tests meant to threaten or intimidate. As soon as they can, those subjected to the character's intimidation – whether or not it is successful – will report him or her to the Town Watch (or similar authorities) as a suspected abomination.

BLOODTHIRST

The character has a thirst for blood, easily awoken and hard to quench. The thirst appears if he or she takes damage and means that the character will not spare any enemies – not even if they surrender. Trying to spare an enemy requires an almost overpowering effort; it requires the character to sacrifice an *Experience* point and then pass a *Vigilant* test.

CODE OF HONOR

The character has adopted a very strict code of honor, applicable in all situations but especially burdensome in combat. The effect of the code is that the player character never runs from a fight which has begun. Sure, sometimes combat can be avoided, but when the fight is on, all enemies must fall!

DARK SECRET

The character has some kind of dark secret, which threatens to destroy his or her reputation and life if revealed. Maybe the character has been a member of a corrupted cult, killed someone, or protected a murderer and never gotten caught. Should the dark secret become publicly known, the character gets one of the burdens *Pariah* or *Wanted* instead, depending on the secret. Once per adventure there is a risk for exposure; the character must roll a *Discreet* test during each adventure, a test with a second chance to succeed. If failed, someone discovers a clue which can lead to the truth. Maybe some kind of physical evidence surfaces (a letter, for instance)? Is it a witness claiming to have seen something or is the character talking in his sleep? Whether the suspicious person is a non-player character or a character, the one with the dark secret must lay their curiosity to rest or suffer the consequences.

Note that a non-player character may want to extort, rather than expose, the character.

ELDERLY

The character is past its prime and has both good and bad days. If the first success test of the day is a success, it is a good day and everything seems to be alright; if the first test of the day is a failure, it is a bad day - the gout sets in, all joints are aching or the character is out of breath even when seated. Whatever the cause, the character has –1 on all tests for the day.

EPILEPTIC

The character is afflicted by a sensitive mind, meaning that he or she can be exposed to violent cramps throughout the body when excited or stressed. If rolling a 20 on a success test the cramping starts and the character is down and out for 1D6 turns. Afterward, he or she is exhausted and suffers –1 on all success tests until the end of the scene.

Pariah as a Burden

The trait *Pariah* from the *Core Rulebook* is a burden and is now counted as such. Player characters who have this trait gain 5 more *Experience* when starting the game, to be spent on a boon, saved for later or used to re-roll tests.

IMPULSIVE

The character acts before thinking. This means that as soon as the player opens his or her mouth and says that the character does something, it does – and the player cannot have second thoughts. The only way to restrain the character is to sacrifice an *Experience* point or accept one (1) permanent corruption.

NIGHTMARES

The character is haunted by nightmares each and every night, possibly because of something he or she has experienced, or for more abstruse reasons, such as an ominous omen or the consequence of a family curse. Each night, the character must pass a *Resolute* test in order to heal naturally, or no healing will occur that day. Other forms of healing are not affected.

MYSTICAL MARK

The character has a mystical mark somewhere on his or her body, maybe a birth mark or a scar gained later in life. Whatever the origin, the character is at risk of being mistaken for having a blight-mark. In situations when it is relevant, the character must pass a test against [Discreet←Vigilant] or attract the attention of a pitch-fork wielding mob or a more or less dangerous witchhunter.

PROTÉGÉ

The character has to put up with and protect a protégé. The protégé can be a beloved child, an elderly but respected mentor, a soulmate or just an annoying relative whose welfare is connected to a future inheritance for the character. Either way, this person is played by the Game Master and tends to get into trouble. The protégé has no stats besides those associated with weak resistance, and gains no *Experience* from adventuring – he or she is as much a burden over time, as at the start.

If the protégé dies or goes missing, the character is afflicted by other problems; sorrow and remorse, mirrored in a suitable burden. If the character protected the person from love, burdens like *Addiction* or *Nightmares* can be appropriate. And if the protection was related to personal gains, maybe *Wanted* or *Arch Enemy* is better – the relatives of the protégé do not easily forget the characters betrayal.

SICKLY

The character suffers from a chronic disease, making him or her weak. Normally, this does not show, but when damaged or traumatized the character is at great risk of dying – all death tests are made with two dice and the worst, most unfavorable outcome stands.

SLOW

The creature or person moves at an unusually slow speed. In situations where precision counts, the movement is 7 meters per turn. In connection to the rule on Flight & Hunt (page 102), the trait gives a –3 *Quick* penalty.

WANTED

The character is wanted for a serious crime, either justly or falsely accused. The effect is that he or she risks getting recognized and hunted. Once per adventure, the character must pass a *Discreet* test to avoid being identified.

he pool of blood spread across the floor around Jela; Kasimer pressed his strong hands against her wound to stop the bleeding. Gormyx leaned against the door, trying to keep it closed, and by the troll's side was Agniesha, seated on the floor, hugging her rune staff, exhausted. Arron lay dead in the corridor outside. There was no point in fighting anymore; the bone crafts of the false cleric would soon breach the door.

Sarli, the group's cadaver-like employer, seemed unaffected by the mess, maybe because she was already dead. She gazed through the cracks in the door. *"We hit them from behind."* She turned to Gormyx: *"You won't enjoy the ride."*

The troll muttered and adjusted his helmet. Agniesha stood up, supported by her staff, and Jela removed Kasimer's hands, replacing them with her own. *"Go,"* she whispered. The dwarf nodded and kissed her forehead.

Sarli drew her sword and cleaved the air in front of her. She entered through the rift to the Yonderworld and pulled the troll with her. The opening collapsed behind them.

Jela felt the world around her grow darker. As if in a dream, she saw the door collapse. Agniesha smashed through the floor before her with a single thrust of her staff and the bone-crafted acolytes that charged into the room tumbled down the hole. From somewhere further away came the war song of Gormyx.

The last thing Jela perceived before darkness took her was Kasimer jumping the hole and attacking the dark priest with his two axes.

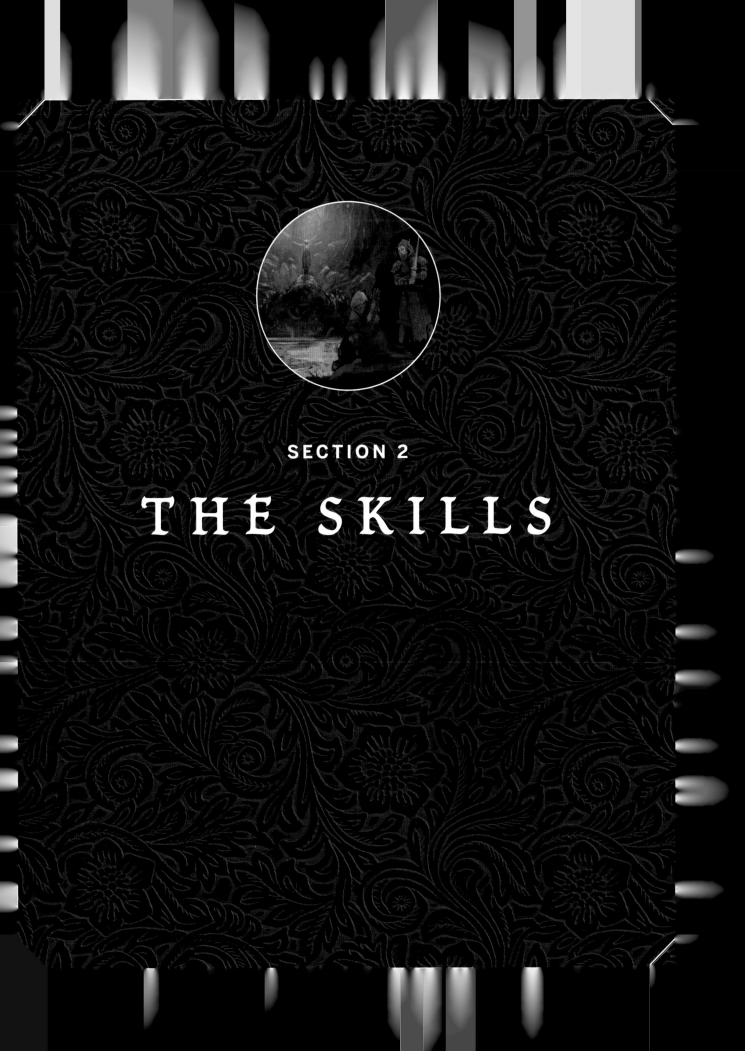

SECTION 2

THE SKILLS

Abilities

HERE YOU WILL FIND descriptions of a long list of abilities, primarily ones connected to the new occupations introduced in this book. Just like with the abilities featured in the *Core Rulebook*, many of them can be acquired by anyone, occupations and archetypes aside. But there are also the archetypical abilities and the abilities linked to the professions, the latter only available once the character lives up to the requirements of a profession – provided that your group agrees with this limitation, that is...

ALCHEMY (EXPANDED)

The alchemists' field of knowledge is constantly growing as old recipes are recovered and new formulas created. With the *Advanced Player's Guide* alchemists may create more elixirs, all of them listed in the margin on page 62, sorted into separate levels like in the *Core Rulebook*. The effects of the elixirs are described in the chapter Equipment on page 120.

Alchemists are used to working with explosive and volatile substances, and are therefore able to handle alchemical grenades correctly and efficiently. Hence, alchemists – starting at the novice level – do not risk failing catastrophically with alchemical grenades.

AGILE COMBAT

Only available to Iron Sworn

During combat in wooded areas and hilly terrain the distance between opponents can shift quickly, from ranged to melee. The Iron Sworn have developed techniques for handling these rapid shifts between weapon types, and the most skilled among them can dance forth over the battlefield, seamlessly alternating between melee and ranged weapons and using every hostile attack for making counter-strikes. The character is trained in the Iron Sworns' advanced techniques on how to emerge victorious from skirmishes.

Novice	**Passive.** The character can split his or her movement and perform one part of the movement action before the combat action, and the other part after. This is done in order to make maximum use of the terrain and cover. The character still suffers Free Attacks from enemies if the movement leads into or through melee combat distance.
Adept	**Passive.** As a part of its combat action, the character may freely switch between weapons. This only pertains to changing weapons; it does not provide an extra action to be used for anything else.
	For instance, the Iron Sworn may start holding two weapons, move a part of its movement range, and as a combat action switch to a bow, fire it, and then switch back to two weapons. Finally, the rest of the movement is made.
Master	**Reaction.** The character gains a second chance to pass all *Defense* tests against

NOVICE ELIXIRS

Alchemical Mine (weak)
Antidote (weak)
Fire Dye
Flash Powder
Herbal Cure
Homing Arrow
Homunculus
Poison (weak)
Purple Sap (weak)
Revealing Light
Stun Bolt
War Paint
Way Bread
Wild Chew

ADEPT ELIXIRS

Alchemical Grenade
Alchemical Mine (moderate)
Antidote (moderate)
Antidote Candle (weak)
Choking Spores
Concentrated Magic
Drone Dew
Eye Drops
Elemental Essence
Ghost Candle
Holy Water
Poison (moderate)
Poison Candle (weak)
Protective Oil
Purple Sap (moderate)
Shadow Tint
Smoke Bomb
Thorn Beasties

MASTER ELIXIRS

Alchemical Mine (strong)
Antidote (strong)
Antidote Candle (moderate)
Elixir of Life
Poison (strong)
Poison Candle (moderate)
Purple Sap (strong)
Spirit Friend
Spore Bomb
Thunder Ball
Transforming Draught
Twilight Tincture
Wraith Dust

Free Attacks provoked by withdrawing from melee. In addition, every such Free Attack against the character lets the Iron Sworn make their own Free Attack against the enemy. The character may freely switch weapons for these counter-strikes and choose the tool that fits the situation best.

ARMORED MYSTIC

Only available to Templars

The templars have developed techniques for performing the miracles of Prios while wearing full armor. When the Knights of the Dying Sun storm some settlement full of heretics or dark spawn, it is far from uncommon to see them blast their enemies and bless their allies while clothed in steel.

Novice	**Passive.** The character's mystical powers are not affected by wearing medium armor. The armor affects *Defense* as usual.
Adept	**Passive.** The character's mystical powers are not affected by wearing heavy armor. The armor affects *Defense* as usual.
Master	**Passive.** The armored mystic has transcended the limitations of the armor, and may instead benefit from it. A +1D4 bonus is added to the armor's protection value when the mystic wears it, since mystical energies flow through the steel.

ARROW JAB

In the chaos of the battlefield, archers sometimes find themselves dragged into the melee. To handle this, techniques on how to use ranged weapons at close range have been developed. This ability may be used with any kind of bow or crossbow.

Novice	**Reaction.** As a reaction to a melee attack against him or her, the character can draw an arrow and use it to stab an enemy. The character must succeed with a normal attack roll against the enemy; a successful hit deals 1D6 damage and the qualities of the projectile (if any) are counted.
Adept	**Reaction.** Like the novice level, but 1D8 damage.
Master	**Reaction.** Like the adept level, but the master also gains a Free Attack with the bow if the jab attack hits. The master stabs with the projectile, then (if successful) loads the bow to make a normal ranged attack at the target. If using a crossbow, this requires that it already be loaded and that the initial stab is made with another bolt, or that the character is in possession of a repeating crossbow.

ARTIFACT CRAFTING

Only available to Artifact Crafters

The glory days of artifact crafting seem to have passed and the powerful secrets of the old rune smiths are lost. However, even in the shadow of the growing corruption, the creative arts still linger on, if in a more modest way. The character is trained in the art of artifact crafting and can create artifacts of the lower order. Higher artifacts can nowadays only be found while excavating Symbaroum's ruins, but artifact crafters belong to a tradition that still holds its head high, in spite of shadows and darkness.

The character is also knowledgeable about legendary artifacts and can discern how artifacts work. *Artifact Crafting* corresponds to the ability *Loremaster* when analyzing artifacts, but it does not affect the use of them.

The artifacts are described in detail in the Equipment chapter, page 123-127

Novice	**Once per adventure.** With a passed *Cunning* test, the character can craft one novice level artifact.
Adept	**Once per adventure.** As an acknowledged artifact crafter, a passed *Cunning* test lets the character craft one adept level artifact.
Master	**Once per adventure.** As a famous artifact crafter, a passed *Cunning* test lets the character craft one master level artifact.

AXE ARTIST

By tradition, many warriors of barbarian origin carry axes into battle, and among these fighters special techniques have been developed – techniques which make full use of the axe's potential. In the hands of the character, the axe is an effective tool of combat.

The weapon used must be an axe of either heavy or single-handed model

Novice	**Active.** The first thing an axe artist learns is to strike with the short-end of the axe in order to induce distracting pain before a mightier blow. The short-end thrust deals 1D6 damage and stuns the enemy if the character passes a *[Accurate←Resolute]* test, meaning that the character gets to make an immediate Free Attack.
Adept	**Active.** Next up is learning the powerful double-strike: to strike with one side of the axe and then follow up by striking a blow with the other. The character makes two attacks in one combat action, both of them at one dice tier lower than normal (1D10=1D8).

Master | **Passive.** The axe master returns to the heart of axe fighting, the mighty blow. Every hit with the axe deals +1D4 damage, limited to one hit per combat action.

BLACKSMITH

All peoples in Ambria and Davokar have their blacksmiths, which says something about their importance. Master smiths are revered in all cultures, but especially among Ambrians and trolls.

The cost of crafting objects is half of the listed price and if the blacksmith later sells the item, he or she gets the list price in payment. In other words, the profit made by the blacksmith is half the listed price.

This ability may be used once per adventure, preferably during a quiet interlude (or between adventures if that seems more reasonable). Should the item be of a consumable nature (like arrows or bolts), the blacksmith can forge 10 copies at a time.

Novice | **Special.** With a passed *Cunning* test, the character can make a novice item. The character can also patch damaged armor or adapt armor to fit creatures of larger or smaller sizes. Novice items are all ordinary weapons and armor, including those with the qualities Short and Long. No other qualities can be crafted by the novice smith.

Adept | **Special.** With a passed *Cunning* test, the character can make an adept item, featuring one quality besides Short or Long. All weapons and armor mentioned in the *Core Rulebook* and the *Advanced Player's Guide* can be crafted by the adept, except items with mystical qualities and those that have more than one quality besides Short or Long. Note that the adept cannot remove negative qualities from items.

Master | **Special.** With a passed *Cunning* test, the character can make a master item. Master Blacksmiths have the capability to add several qualities to weapons and armor, and also to remove negative qualities. Adding to that, they may instill mystical qualities into all kinds of weapons and armor. For each added or removed quality, the list price of the item is cumulatively increased by ×5. Mystical qualities increase the value by ×10.

BLOOD COMBAT
Only available to Wrath Guard

The witches on Karvosti understand the power of the blood better than others. These insights have been developed in cooperation with the Guard of

---

During Adventures or Between Them?

Some abilities can be used "once per adventure." This can be handled in two ways, depending on what the gaming group prefers. If the characters also have active periods in-between adventures, where they engage in various activities (working, running a business or something like that), these abilities may be rolled during that time frame; some characters spend the down-time in their laboratory, their smithy and so on. If the group is totally committed to continuous adventuring it may be necessary to roll for these abilities at the start of each new adventure, or to find a practical situation during the adventure.

---

the Slumbering Wrath. The dedication and training of the guard allows them to use the power of spilled blood to their own advantage in combat – whether the blood is theirs or the enemy's.

Novice | **Reaction.** The character draws strength from the blood it spills. When his or her *Toughness* has been halved, the character gains a second chance to succeed with all attack tests in melee combat.

Adept | **Reaction.** The character's hits grow more powerful the more damaged he or she is; when *Toughness* has been more than halved, all attacks made by the character in melee combat deal an additional +1D8 in damage.

Master | **Reaction.** The warrior is healed by the blood spilled by the enemy; half of the damage that the character deals in melee combat is added to the character's *Toughness*, rounded down.

CHANNELING

Some sorcerers and cultists have through exposure to dark powers developed a capacity to endure corruption and to attract corruption that would have affected others. With practice, *Channeling* may also be used for passing corruption on to others, as a brutal weapon.

Novice | **Reaction.** The character can choose to receive temporary corruption that will otherwise affect someone else within sight.

Adept | **Reaction.** The character gets a second chance when rolling for corruption and in situations when receiving corruption for someone else. The character may accept the higher or lower outcome depending on what is more favorable; combined with the master level in Channeling the higher outcome is better, in all other cases the lower outcome is preferable.

Master **Reaction.** The character can pass corruption on to someone else; this is true for all forms of corruption he or she suffers, no matter the source. With a successful [Resolute←Resolute] test, corruption suffered is transferred to a target in sight. If the test fails, the master still only suffers half of the corruption (rounded up), while the rest leaks out into the surrounding area, making plants wither and the ground darken.

CHEAP SHOT

In the slums of Alberetor's larger cities, special techniques for self-defense emerged. These techniques are still practiced among the gangs of Yndaros.

Novice **Active.** Cheap Shots like a "gutter-kiss" (head-butt) or a "goblin-squeeze" (groin kick) comes naturally to the character in stressful situations. Such an attack deals 1D6 damage, and if the opponent is damaged the character also gains a Free Attack against him or her.

Adept **Reaction.** The character performs a normal melee attack and if it deals damage, he or she adds a trip or a tackle. Such a maneuver knocks the opponent to the ground if the character succeeds with a [Cunning←Quick] test.

Master **Reaction.** Every enemy who engages the character in melee suffers a bloody riposte directly after each attack, dealing 1D6 damage if successful. The riposte always hits a weak spot and consequently ignores any *Armor*.

ENSNARE

Using weapons like bolas, nets or the long whip, many fighters and hunters of barbarian origin learn to limit the movement of enemies or prey. This skill is also known among Ambrians; flail weapons are, for instance, used in the lengthy show-fights at the gladiatorial arenas and by many bounty hunters. Abducted humans can sometimes be seen wielding chain staffs, making it possible to ensnare the enemy. The character is trained in the ensnaring techniques used to gain *Advantage* in melee or to capture prey alive.

Novice **Active.** The character gains a second chance to ensnare a target (requires a weapon with the quality Ensnaring, see page 118).

Adept **Active.** In addition to the novice effect, the character gains a second chance to bring down an ensnared enemy (requires a weapon with the quality Ensnaring, see page 118).

Master **Reaction.** The character's skill with ensnaring weapons is such that every ensnaring attack hits the target's neck and has a strangling effect; besides the ensnaring effect and the chance to bring down the enemy, the target suffers 1D6 damage per turn, ignoring armor. If the target reaches 0 *Toughness*, the character can choose to make it unconscious instead of dead/dying.

FEAT OF STRENGTH
Only available to Warriors

The warrior's spirit is strengthened in combat, giving him or her miraculous power when needed. The character is one of those who have found this source of aggression within, and know how to make use of it.

Novice **Passive.** The character can handle taking a beating and counts *Toughness* as [Strong +5]. This does not affect the *Pain Threshold*, which is based on *Strong/2* as usual.

Adept **Reaction.** The character grows stronger by suffering damage. When the character's *Toughness* is halved, he has a second chance to pass all tests against *Strong*, including attacks if rolled against *Strong*.

Master **Reaction.** The character grows even stronger when severely damaged. When the character's *Toughness* is halved, he or she deals +1D4 melee damage, in addition to the effect mentioned at the adept level.

FLAILER

Among Ambria's knights and their squires, the efficiency of jointed chain-weapons has long been known. New ways of using jointed weapons have emerged on the battlefield, and these techniques have been passed on to other warriors. The character has studied the secrets of the jointed weapons and learned to make full use of their potential.

Novice **Passive.** In the character's hands, a jointed weapon gains the quality Ensnaring, and may therefore be used to ensnare an enemy, instead of for making a normal attack.

Adept **Passive.** The character can put great force into the secondary damage of jointed weapons; such hits now deal 1D8 damage, instead of 1D6.

Master **Active.** The master flailer can use a jointed weapon to continue to strike even after hav-

Table 3: Abilities

ABILITY	ARCHETYPE/OCCUPATION
Acrobatics	Warrior, Rogue
Alchemy	Mystic, Rogue
Agile Combat	**Iron Sworn only**
Armored Mystic	**Templar only**
Arrow Jab	Hunter
Artifact Crafting	**Artifact Crafter only**
Axe Artist	Warrior
Backstab	Rogue
Beast Lore	Mystic, Rogue
Berserker	Warrior
Blacksmith	All
Blood Combat	**Wrath Guard only**
Bodyguard	Warrior
Channeling	Mystic, Rogue
Cheap Shot	Rogue
Dominate	Warrior, Mystic, Rogue
Ensnare	Warrior, Rogue
Equestrian	Warrior, Mystic, Rogue
Exceptional Attribute	Warrior, Mystic, Rogue
Feat of Strength	**Warrior only**
Feint	Rogue
Flailer	Warrior
Hammer Rhythm	Warrior
Hunter's Instinct	**Hunter only**
Iron Fist	Warrior
Knife Play	Rogue
Leader	Warrior, Mystic, Rogue
Loremaster	Mystic, Rogue
Man-at-arms	Warrior
Mantle Dance	**Gentleman Thief only**
Marksman	Warrior, Rogue
Medicus	Mystic, Rogue
Mystical Power	Mystic
Natural Warrior	Warrior

ABILITY	ARCHETYPE/OCCUPATION
Opportunist	Warrior, Rogue
Poisoner	Mystic, Rogue
Polearm Mastery	Warrior, Rogue
Pyrotechnics	**Queen's Spy only**
Quick Draw	Warrior, Rogue
Rapid Fire	Hunter, Rogue
Rapid Reflexes	**Rogue only**
Recovery	Warrior, Mystic, Rogue
Ritualist	Warrior, Mystic, Rogue
Rune Tattoo	Warrior
Shield Fighter	Warrior
Siege Expert	All
Sixth Sense	Warrior, Rogue
Sorcery	Mystic
Staff Fighting	Hunter, Warrior
Staff Magic	**Staff Mage only**
Steadfast	Warrior, Mystic, Rogue
Steel Throw	Warrior, Rogue
Strangler	Rogue
Strong Gift	**Mystic only**
Sword Saint	Warrior
Symbolism	Mystic
Tactician	Mystic, Rogue
Theurgy	Mystic
Trapper	Hunter, Rogue
Trick Archery	Hunter
Troll Singing	Mystic
Twin Attack	Warrior, Rogue
Two-handed Force	Warrior
Witchcraft	Mystic
Witchsight	Mystic, Rogue
Wizardry	Mystic
Wrestling	Warrior

ing hit a target. The character may perform attacks against all enemies within range of melee; each attack is rolled separately.

HAMMER RHYTHM

As a weapon, the hammer is ancient and its brutal simplicity may in the right hands pound forth a deadly rhythm echoing over the battlefield.

The character is one of those who, through training and experience, can utilize the force of the hammer, whether in its single-handed or heavy version.

Novice	**Reaction.** The character can crush the enemy's shield with the hammer. After a failed attack roll where the opponent defends with a shield (that is, the enemy parries the character's attack), the character may roll a *[Strong←Quick]*. If successful, a wooden shield shatters to splinters while a metal shield is torn from the opponent's arm and dropped. The shield carrier also suffers 1D6 damage from the heavy blow.
Adept	**Reaction.** When an enemy successfully defends against a hammer attack, the character can grip the shaft of the hammer with both hands and use it to ram the enemy. A passed *[Strong←Strong]* test drives the opponent one step backwards, and in the space that opens up, the adept hammer fighter gets to make a Free Attack against the enemy.
Master	**Active.** The character makes two hammer attacks against the same target, in one action. If the victim successfully defends against any of these, the master may perform a hammer ram as described at the adept level. Only one ramming per turn is allowed, even if the opponent defends against both attacks.

HUNTER'S INSTINCT
Only available to Hunters

Hunters have a finely tuned instinct and when it comes down to it there are few targets – be they criminal, beast or sorcerer – who can avoid the hunter's projectiles.

Novice	**Special.** The hunter appoints a target in sight and gets a second chance to succeed with all ranged attacks against it. The target is appointed when the character makes an attack against it, and the effect lasts till the prey dies or the scene ends.
Adept	**Passive.** The hunter's ranged attacks against an appointed target deal +1D4 damage.
Master	**Reaction.** The master hunter lets no prey escape. The character gets a ranged Free Attack at an appointed target as soon as it moves. This happens every time the target uses a movement action to get from one place to another; a target using both actions for movement provokes two ranged Free Attacks from the character.

KNIFE PLAY

The use of knives is common in the slums of Yndaros; short blades have advantages when fighting in narrow alleys, down in the drain-tunnels or inside buildings. A special fighting technique has emerged from this, commonly called *Knife Play*. The skills have spread across Ambria to be employed wherever combat is waged in restricted spaces.

Knife Play may only be performed with knife-like weapons, i.e. sticking or cutting weapons with the quality Short.

Novice	**Passive.** The character can choose to attack with *Quick* instead of *Accurate* when attacking with a short, knife-like weapon.
Adept	**Passive.** The character makes two separate knife-attacks at the same target with every combat action. If the character also has Twin Attack, this ability only affects one of the attacks, for a total of three attacks (two with the main hand and one with the other).
Master	**Reaction.** The character can fight effectively with a knife at very short range from the enemy: when the character deals damage with a knife-attack, he or she is assumed to be so close that the enemy has a hard time using ordinary weapons effectively (the character has two chances to pass the *Defense* test), and is unable to attack with Long weapons. To reach a better distance, the enemy has to... ... win the initiative next turn (see Quick Strike on page 99 or Take the Initiative on page 104) and then continue attacking until the knife-fighter hits again. ... use a movement action to withdraw from melee, and then suffer a Free Attack from the knife-fighter. If the Free Attack deals damage, the enemy once again finds itself at too short of a distance to attack effectively.

MANTLE DANCE
Only available to Gentleman Thief

Among Ambria's fencers, shields are regarded as awkward and barbaric, making the parrying dagger a more fashionable tool for defense. Another school has gone one step further and developed elegant techniques that turn the fencer's mantle into a dancing shield.

The character may use his or her free hand along with a mantle or similar sheet of cloth in *Defense*. When used by the character, the sheet becomes a sweeping and hypnotic shield that can confuse or temporarily blind the opponent.

Novice	**Passive.** The character's mantle, or some similar sheet of cloth held in the hand, gives a +1 bonus to *Defense*.
Adept	**Active.** The mantle strikes at the enemy's eyes, temporarily blinding the target if the attack roll is successful. The character immediately gains a Free Attack against the target, an attack that the enemy must defend against as if blinded. Everyone attacking the blind target can take advantage of the situation for the duration of one turn.
Master	**Active.** In the master's hands, the mantle is like a whip with the quality Ensnaring, making it possible to use it to trap the target. See the quality Ensnaring on page 118 for details.

OPPORTUNIST

In the midst of battle, weak spots are exposed and can be exploited. This fact is known to experienced warriors in both Ambria and Davokar, who have taught others how to make use of such opportunities.

Novice	**Reaction.** The character has a second chance to succeed on Free Attacks gained from the enemy withdrawing from melee.
Adept	**Reaction.** The character may use active abilities on Free Attacks gained from the enemy withdrawing from melee. If used, this cancels out the second chance to succeed granted by the novice level.
Master	**Reaction.** When an enemy withdraws from melee, the master opportunist both gains a second chance to succeed with and is allowed to use active abilities on the Free Attack roll.

PYROTECHNICS
Only available to Queen's Spy
In Ambria, advances within the field of alchemy have led to the use of alchemical weapons. The secret agents of the Queen are known to employ such devices when combating the enemies of the realm or escaping from hazardous situations. The character can use special elixirs to blind or otherwise weaken the enemy. Note that the master

level of the ability *Sixth Sense* makes it possible to act normally despite being blinded; *Sixth Sense* does not affect any other effects from *Pyrotechnics*.

Novice	**Active.** The character can use Flash Powder created by an alchemist to dazzle an opponent in melee combat. This requires an *[Accurate←Quick]* test; the attack deals 1D4 damage (ignoring armor) and the target is blinded for 1D4 turns. The character can also handle alchemical grenades and alchemical mines without risking a catastrophic failure.
Adept	**Active.** The character can use an alchemical Smoke Bomb correctly to fill an area with dense smoke. If the Smoke Bomb is thrown at a distance, an *Accurate* test is needed for it to land where intended. If dropped at the character's feet no test is needed, but the character is affected just like all others in the vicinity. Everyone in the area, friends and enemies, are blinded until they leave the place (two movement actions in any direction). Those remaining in the smoke must pass a *Strong* test each turn or suffer 1D4 damage, ignoring armor, from smoke poisoning.
Master	**Active.** The character can effectively activate and throw an alchemical Thunder Ball at a group of enemies. All targets within a radius of five meters are hit, an *[Accurate←Quick]* test decides if they suffer whole or half damage. The damage is 1D12, ignoring armor. Furthermore, all targets suffering from the full effect are blinded for 1D4 turns.

RAPID FIRE
Archers in Ambria and Davokar have developed techniques for rapid firing. In essence, if right-handed, they place the arrow on the right side of the bow instead of on the left, and draw several arrows at a time from the quiver to hold them in the left hand. This way, arrows may be knocked, aimed and fired in a single motion, meaning that they can be launched one after the other – truly bad news for poorly armored targets.

The ability requires that some kind of bow be used in combat.

Novice	**Active.** The character can sacrifice his or her movement action to fire a second arrow, two in total. This may only be done if the combat action is also used for firing a bow. The arrows are rolled separately and may (but do not have to) be aimed at the same target.

| Adept | **Active.** The character may fire two arrows with a single combat action, at one or two different targets. |
| Master | **Active.** The character fires three arrows with a single combat action, at one or different targets. |

RAPID REFLEXES
Only available to Rogues

Rogues do not have much in common, besides that they all are survivalists – either because they are quite fond of being alive or in order for them to keep striving for their goals. This will to stay alive has resulted in the development of various ways to avoid being damaged.

Novice	**Reaction.** In situations when the character suffers from an effect which may result in full or half damage (for instance from alchemical grenades and Brimstone Cascade), the character suffers half damage instead of full, and no damage instead of half. As an example, if hit by a Brimstone Cascade that normally deals 1D12 with a hit and 1D6 with a miss, this is transformed into 1D6 with a hit and no damage at all with a miss.
Adept	**Reaction.** The rogue avoids the enemy's melee attack and dances around to its back; with a passed *Defense* test, the rogue and the enemy switch places, if the player wishes. This means that the rogue gets away from being flanked without suffering a Free Attack, and also that the enemy ends up in a flanked position if there was an ally standing next to the rogue.
Master	**Passive.** The expert rogue's reflexes are so finely tuned that he or she ignores the usual turn order and always acts first; only others with this ability and a higher value in *Quick* or *Vigilant* gets to go before the rogue.

RUNE TATTOO

The rune crafters of Clan Vajvod in eastern Davokar often tattoo themselves and their allies with powerful runes. These runes seem almost alive and glow red-hot when activated in combat. The character carries such tattoos, either self-made (requires the ritual *Carve Rune Tattoo*) or granted to the character as a gift or a reward, likely for a service of great importance for the symbolist who made it.

Rune Tattoo requires that someone uses the ritual *Carve Rune Tattoo* on the character. If the character has the ability from the start, the tattoo is already in place.

| Novice | **Reaction.** The rune tattoo provides a +1D4 bonus to armor against attacks, but only if the character chooses to activate it. Activating the effect costs one temporary corruption for each attack that hits and the character decides whether or not to use it before he or she rolls for other kinds of armor.

In addition, the rune protects from weather and wind like a full set of clothes. |
| Adept | **Free.** The rune tattoo is attracted to injuries on the character's body and glows around the wounds. The character regenerates one point of *Toughness* per turn; each point healed costs one point in temporary corruption. The tattooed warrior may abort the regeneration process when he or she wishes. |
| Master | **Reaction.** The rune tattoo adds power to the warrior's attacks. When an enemy is hit and the character so wishes, the glowing tattoo flows over the weapon dealing +1D4 damage, at the cost of as many points in temporary corruption for the character. |

SIEGE EXPERT

In Ambria, wars are fought in two ways: on the battlefield and through sieges. Siege weapons are used in both cases. This ability covers the use of ballistae, siege towers and catapults, and also the skill to construct these contraptions from the ground up. A siege expert can plan and organize the digging of protective trenches and tunnels for the purpose of undermining an enemy's walls. Added to this is the use of alchemical battlefield weapons: alchemical grenades, breaching pots, missile batteries and alchemical fire tubes, both stationary and portable.

All siege and battlefield weapons are described in the Weapons' section, starting on page 110.

| Novice | **Special.** The character is trained to use a ballista and to construct siege towers on location. The character can handle alchemical grenades and does not risk them detonating by mistake, like an inexperienced user must worry about. |
| Adept | **Special.** The character can lead the work when building and then effectively use more advanced siege weapons, like the catapult and its bigger cousin, the trebuchet. At the site of a siege, the character can plan and lead the work of digging protective trenches and undermining tunnels. The character has learned the deeper secrets regarding the art of siege weapons – alchemical smoke bombs hiding attacking troops from hostile archers; the use of the alchemical |

breaching pot that blasts holes in the enemy's fortifications; and the alchemical fire tube, spewing fire and death at anyone passing in front of it. Also, the portable version of the alchemical fire tube can safely be handled under stress, without risking catastrophic failures.

Master **Special.** The character's understanding of alchemical weapons is exceptional, and they all get the quality Massive if they do not have it already.

STAFF FIGHTING

The apparent simplicity of the staff tends to mask its versatility as a weapon, which is demonstrated by skilled staff fighters, often found among Davokar's elves and the ascetic staff mages who use their rune staffs for fighting if the situation demands it. There are also staff fighters among the barbarians, often using the Pike Axe as a weapon (the same weapon called a Halberd in Ambria). The question of whether or not these fighting traditions have a common origin is redundant; they are all equally effective – something a character with this ability will be able to demonstrate.

Staff Fighting may be performed with all Long weapons – staff, spear, halberd and pike. Also the more exotic Chain Staff can be used. Moreover, staff fighting techniques are especially useful for anyone using them with the simplest of all Long weapons – the wooden staff.

Novice **Passive.** The character is trained to parry incoming attacks and gains +1 in *Defense*; with the simple wooden staff or a rune staff – quicker and better balanced than other weapons in the category – the bonus is +2 in *Defense*.

Adept **Reaction.** The character uses the back end of the Long weapon to gain a Free Attack if the opponent defends against the initial attack. The Free Attack is rolled separately and the damage is 1D6.

If armed with a wooden staff (that is, not a spear or a halberd, but including rune staffs), this may also be done after every successful *Defense* against melee attacks while holding the weapon – the staff fighter makes a quick riposte after having parried.

Master **Active.** The character has learned how to target the legs and then attack the fallen enemy with a single motion. The initial attack sends the enemy to the ground if the attacker succeeds with a *[Accurate←Quick]* test and the follow-up is performed as a Free Attack with *Advantage* on the opponent.

STAFF MAGIC
Only available to Staff Mages

The staff mages were once the guards of the Symbarian emperor. After the fall of the last emperor, they retreated to their castle deep inside Davokar, hoping to reform their weakened order. To them, they were to blame for the fall of Symbaroum; they failed in their duty because they focused more on titles, intrigues and status than on protecting the empire.

The reformation gave birth to the order as it is today, its members appearing as simply dressed and taciturn mystics with astounding powers. The character is one of the chosen, given a rune staff and the task of restoring the former grandeur of the order by crushing the darkness and placing the rightful heir of the last emperor on the Throne of Thorns in Symbar.

The staff mages are an elite order, placing high demands on recruits from the start; only the most promising mystics can ever hope to battle darkness as members of their order.

Novice   **Special.** The staff mage binds his or her soul to a rune staff, carved with the runes of the elements. The staff absorbs all corruption the character would have gained by learning the powers of the tradition at the novice level. If the character already has permanent corruption when being bound to the staff, the level of permanent corruption is reduced by 1D6. This can only be done once; if the staff gets lost or must be replaced, no additional reduction is made.

          In addition, as a free action the staff mage can activate an elemental rune and then deal +1D4 damage with the staff, no matter if it is used in combination with the powers of the tradition or as a melee weapon. The character can chose between fire, lightning, cold or acid. Activating the rune gives no corruption.

Adept   **Special.** The staff absorbs all corruption the character would have gained by learning the powers of the tradition at the adept level. Also, the staff binds the corruption so well that the character gets a second chance to roll for corruption when using all powers included in the tradition; the character suffers from the lower of the two outcomes.

Master   **Special.** The staff absorbs all corruption the character would have gained by learning the powers of the tradition at the master level. The staff also binds temporary corruption so effectively, that the character no longer suffers any temporary corruption when using the powers of staff magic.

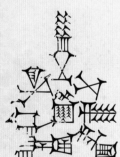

Symbols on parchment that according to Clan Varakko are a map of a shrine from the age of Symbaroum. The adjacent symbols, which mean Deity and Bloodshed, tickle the imagination of many wizards.

STRONG GIFT
Only available to Mystics

There are many myths describing the origin of mystical powers, and all established traditions are quick to state that theirs is the oldest, or at least nearly as old as the mystical practice itself. Whatever the truth may be, many believe that it was self-taught mystics with an especially perfected or strong gift who founded the first traditions.

The *Strong Gift* – innate or acquired through trials and practice – can still be found with some mystics. For one thing, the gift provides a singular resistance against the corruption of the world. It also endows the mystic with the ability to use improvised mystical powers, at a high cost in corruption.

Novice   **Special.** The Strong Gift allows the character to choose a signature power. This power is selected from among the ones already known to the mystic, and that power then only costs one (1) temporary corruption to use. If the character has no powers or just prefers to have a tainting ability as its signature instead, this is also allowed – a gift linked to the ability Ritualist (including all individual rituals) or to Witchsight means that these never cost more than one temporary corruption to use. Also, traits such as *Wisdom of the Ages* may be chosen.

          The Strong Gift has no effect on the cost in permanent corruption for learning a power outside a mystical tradition; it only affects the amount of temporary corruption gained when using it.

Adept   **Passive.** A character with the adept level in Strong Gift uses his or her whole *Resolute* value as the corruption threshold, instead of only half. Such an individual does not become blight born until its total corruption reaches a value of *Resolute* ×2.

Master   **Special.** The gift of the Master lets the character cast any mystical power, albeit only at the novice level. There is a second chance to fail all success tests and using the power causes 1D8 temporary corruption. All mystical powers are available, no matter what tradition they belong to.

SWORD SAINT

Among Ambria's duelists, there are those who have achieved an almost mystic symbiosis with their fencing swords, who handle their weapons as if they were extensions of their body and soul. The *Sword Saint* techniques may only be used with a fencing sword (or other single-handed sword with the quality Precise). A parrying dagger or the ability *Mantle Dance* may also be used in combination with the sword, but *Sword Saint* cannot be combined with the ability *Twin Attack* to gain additional bonuses to damage.

Novice **Passive.** The character has learned to take full advantage of fighting with a Precise sword in one hand and a parrying dagger in the other. The damage dealt by the sword is 1D10, instead of 1D8.

Adept **Reaction.** The character can perform a rapid riposte. After one successful *Defense* per turn, the character gains a Free Attack against the enemy.

Master **Reaction.** The master can perform a series of ripostes and gains a Free Attack against the opponent with each successful *Defense* test, with no limitation on the number of Free Attacks per turn.

As a Passive addition, the damage of the Precise sword increases to 1D12.

SYMBOLISM

Symbolism was developed in the east, beyond the Ravens, in what the symbolists call *"The first city of humans"* – a place of myth, lost somewhere in the vast deserts of the eastern wastes. Nowadays, the symbolists gather in Vajvod, in eastern Davokar, even though some of them travel far and wide in their search for knowledge of runes, signs and symbols. The basic assumption of the symbolists states that the world consists of signs and symbols, and that it therefore may be affected and influenced by altering signs and symbols which represent its diverse features.

The powers of *Symbolism* are created by drawing or writing. More fanciful procedures are also possible, like embroidery, etchings or weaves. Procedures aside, the power of the symbol is released by the symbolist's command, and the symbol vaporizes when its power has been unleashed.

Creating a symbol gives no corruption but when it is activated the one who uses it suffers one (1) point of temporary corruption.

Novice. **Special.** The character has begun to grasp the power of runes. The signs must be physically represented – carved, painted, etched, tattooed – which takes time; for a novice, it takes one hour to create a power symbol. However, it only takes a combat action to activate a symbol, which is done by uttering an activation phrase. Note that the symbolist has to see or be in direct contact (melee range) with the symbol in order to activate it.

The symbolist can only have one symbol per mystical power prepared in this way. When a symbol has been used it must be recharged, which takes as much time as it does to create the symbol from scratch.

Adept **Special.** With a combat action, the symbolist can quickly paint a symbol in a book or draw it in the mud or dust of the ground. These temporary symbols transcend the limitation stating that the symbolist may only have one symbol per power prepared.

To the adept, activating symbols – no matter if they are prepared in a more permanent fashion (see novice) or are of a temporary nature – is a free action where he or she

The Truth of the Symbolists

According to the symbolists of Clan Vajvod, humans once arrived in the region west of the Ravens as refugees from the east. The legends say that the territory of the Vajvods was the first to be populated and that the colonization cost many lives. Exactly what stood in their way is a topic for debate and guesses – there is talk of giants, hordes of predatory beasts and a human tribe called Aravax or Axerva, possibly related to the spider-like race later known as the followers of Angathal Taar. Irrespective of which, the symbolists claim that the legends have an invaluable lesson to tell.

Sure, lots of single human lives could have been saved if the refugees had used more potent and more quickly crafted mystical powers, but only in the short term. That humankind finally triumphed was due to what had been learned from previous mistakes – insights regarding the world's capacity to brutally punish all who violate or abuse it. Based on this logic, the orthodox symbolists claim that the difference between all other mystical traditions is slim; that witches and wizards in reality are not much better than sorcerers.

Traps and Terrain

The effectiveness of traps is determined by the terrain's limitations and potential. Hence, it is suggested that you use a Combat Map when traps are employed (see page 162 in the *Core Rulebook*). If Movement by Scale is used, a trap covers one square (see page 181 in the *Core Rulebook*).

only has to utter a single word. However, only one symbol may be activated per turn.

In addition, the adept symbolist can choose to activate symbols using a physical trigger instead of a word. The trigger is decided by the mystic when the symbol is created, and can for instance be that a living creature enters a room, that someone steps on the symbol or that a weapon is drawn within melee range. The symbolist may or may not exclude him- or herself from this equation, but the allies of the symbolist cannot be excluded: if they act in accordance with the trigger, the symbol is activated.

The adept can erase one of his or her own symbols with a simple gesture (free action), but this requires actually touching the symbol.

Master **Active.** As a combat action, the symbolist can draw flaming power runes in the air and activate them as part of the same action. Hence, the symbols work just like the powers of other traditions, aside from the mystic only suffering one point in temporary corruption per activation. These momentary symbols transcend the limitation stating that the symbolist may only have one symbol per power prepared.

TRAPPER

Traps have been used since ancient times and in Davokar they are particularly useful. Among barbarians, the art of trap-making is known to many and even Ambrians venturing into the woods know to appreciate a good trap. The character has realized that monsters and abominations are best combated after having been caught and fettered.

Trained trappers can deploy and disarm both mechanical traps and alchemical mines. Furthermore, when the need arises, the character can quickly manufacture improvised traps from materials at hand.

See more on the rules regarding traps on page 102.

Novice **Active.** With a passed *Cunning* test, the character can use a combat action to deploy or disarm a mechanical trap. The effect depends on the level of the trap (see page 127 in the Equipment chapter). The character can also build an improvised trap, but this requires a whole turn to complete. An improvised trap made by the character deals 1D6 damage.

Adept **Active.** The character can handle alchemical mines the same way he or she handles mechanical traps. An improvised trap made by the character now deals 1D8 damage.

Master **Active.** The character is a renowned trapper who knows how to make the most of any kind of trap. Traps and mines are counted as one tier higher: weak becomes moderate, moderate becomes strong and the character gets a second chance on all rolls when using a strong device – the enemies' attempts to discover, disarm or get free become more difficult; also the damage dice is rolled twice and the highest outcome stands. For alchemical traps, the damage re-roll only pertains to the initial explosion, not the ongoing damage that follows. Improvised traps now deal 1D10 damage.

TRICK ARCHERY

Trick shooting with bows and crossbows is highest fashion in Ambria, as appreciated at shows as it is effective in combat. Trick archers are not very many, since most people lack the patience for honing their skills to such an astounding degree. The character is one of the few who have dedicated their lives to mastering the bow or the crossbow.

Novice **Active.** The character can use a full turn (combat plus movement action) to aim perfectly and then hit a very precise location on the enemy; shoot a weapon from a hand, nail a body-part to a nearby wall or tree, or aim for the eyes to blind the enemy. The attack is rolled as usual and if it hits and deals damage, the intended effect also occurs: a weapon is dropped and must be picked up, an arrow that nails the enemy to a wall must be pulled out or broken, and a hit close to the eyes leaves the enemy temporarily blinded. Whichever the case, the target loses a combat action in order to deal with the situation.

Adept **Active.** The archer can cause projectiles to ricochet off floors, walls, furniture, shields or living creatures with robust skin or armor in order to hit targets behind cover so the character does not need free line of sight before firing. He or she must have an idea of where the target is or have watched it duck into hiding, for instance into cover or an adjacent room. If the target has made a double movement action it cannot be hit.

This kind of attack is made as usual, regarding both success test and damage test.

Master **Reaction.** Once per turn, the character can parry a successful attack at range. This ranged parrying maneuver can be of two types:

Versus a melee attack aimed at an ally:
The master archer fires a projectile that deflects an attack which otherwise would have hit one of his or her allies. This parrying maneuver requires a passed *[Accurate←Quick]* test; if successful, the attack misses the ally without dealing any damage.

Versus a physical projectile aimed at the archer or an ally: The parrying maneuver requires a passed *[Accurate←Quick]* test; if successful, the incoming projectile is deflected and misses its target.

TROLL SINGING

The mystical tradition of trolls is expressed through singing, sometimes accompanied by music played on horn, flute or pipes. According to the trolls' educational songs, the tradition stems from the kauking singing style that trolls use to communicate over long distances in the Underworld.

Novice	**Special.** The troll singer suffers no permanent corruption from learning troll song rituals or powers at the novice level, but has no protection from temporary corruption suffered when singing them. In addition, once per scene all troll singers have a second chance to succeed on a test when trying to influence or affect a target's mind (that is, situations when the adversary defends using the attribute *Resolute*). The re-roll may not be used to create or maintain a chain of mystical effects.
Adept	**Special.** The troll singer suffers no permanent corruption from learning troll songs at the adept level. Additionally, the adept may re-roll one success test when trying to influence or affect a target's mind, also when creating or maintaining a chain of such mystical effects.
Master	**Special.** The troll singer suffers no permanent corruption from learning troll songs at the master level. The master may re-roll every success test when trying to influence or affect a target's mind, also when creating or maintaining a chain of such mystical effects.

WRESTLING

Wrestling is popular among warriors, appreciated for educational purposes as well as its entertainment value. Hence, wrestling matches can be seen in the arenas of Ambria's larger towns, in army camps among bored soldiers and on the battlefield amidst swinging swords and axes. The character is trained to wrestle, both with and without the protection of armor.

The trait *Robust* adds a bonus to *Strong* when throwing an opponent or resisting being thrown: +2 at novice level, +4 at adept level, +8 at master level. *Robust* gives no bonus if some other attribute besides *Strong* is used.

Novice	**Active.** The character knows the basic wrestling maneuvers and can use them against armed opponents. Also, the character can wrestle while holding weapons; they need not be dropped or put away. The attack is made as usual and if successful the wrestler gets the enemy in a firm grip. The wrestler may then try to throw the enemy or just maintain the grip; both alternatives require a *[Strong←Strong]* test. The throw inflicts 1D4 damage, ignoring armor, and leaves the enemy flat on its back. The alternative to a throw, maintaining the grip, inflicts no damage, but the enemy cannot act until the wrestler fails a *[Strong←Strong]* test. Also, all allies of the wrestler have *Advantage* on the gripped enemy. The wrestler is unable to do anything else while maintaining the grip, leaving him or her vulnerable: all enemies have *Advantage* on the wrestler.
Adept	**Reaction.** The character has learned how to counter an opponent's strength and can use it to throw the enemy to the ground. First, the wrestler must pass a normal *Defense* test verses the enemy's melee attack, then he or she must pass a *[Quick←Strong]* test. The throw deals 1D4 damage, ignoring armor, and the thrown enemy ends up flat on its back, loses its breath and is unable to perform any active actions during the following turn.
Master	**Reaction.** The reactive throw of the character (see the adept level) only requires a passed *[Quick←Strong]* test, no *Defense* test is needed. If the throw fails, then a *Defense* test is rolled to avoid being hit. The master's throw deals 1D6 damage, ignoring armor, and the thrown enemy ends up flat on its back, loses its breath and is unable to perform any active actions during the following turn. Furthermore, the master wrestler immediately gets a *Free Attack* on the enemy.

Kauking

The singing style known as Kauking among the trolls can be described as a high-pitched, melodic wailing which carries over long distances. The songs are usually wordless, but the tones, melody and rhythm have meaning to those equipped to understand.

Mystical Traditions

THE WORLD IS OLD and its mystical traditions many and varied. Some of these come into contact with Ambria and Davokar; others are already established there, in secrecy in Ambria or existing in remote, seldom visited locations deep inside Davokar – *Staff Magic*, *Symbolism* and *Troll Singing* count among these.

Symbolism

SYMBOLISM WAS BORN in the east, beyond the Ravens, and fleeing mystics brought it to what now is Clan Vajvod's territory in Davokar. The symbolists predate the founding of Clan Vajvod, at least according to the rune-covered remnants that the barbarians discovered when they first came to the area.

Foremost among these remnants is the Azure Temple, built in blue stone brought to Vajvod from beyond the mountains and covered in runes carved by many generations of symbolists. Still today, the blue temple is the scene of the rare Rune Meets, when new members are initiated into the tradition.

THE TITLES OF SYMBOLISM

The symbolists have few titles and only differ between apprentices and initiated members, often called "Followers" and "Weavers". The term "Master Weaver" is also used as an honorary title for

prominent symbolists. The followers are sometimes jokingly called "Spindles," after the spinning tool, since many symbolists think of the world as a weave or painting which they remodel or repaint with their powers. It is also customary for Weavers to take titles they think they deserve – from "Sign Carver," "Fate Painter" and "Pattern Braider," to "Rune Artist" and "Power Crafter." At the Rune Meet, a yearly gathering where symbolists who are able convene at the Azure Temple in Vojvodar, only Weavers may speak and vote, while Followers listen. Master Weavers have no special authority besides that which is granted to all Weavers, but naturally their opinions carry extra weight.

POWERS

Symbolists paint or write when using powers, often on perishable materials like parchment or in the dirt, but skilled Weavers can write glowing runes

A staff mage knows about the same regarding Davokar's and Symbaroum's fate as other mystics and knowledgeable treasure hunters do. They know of relatively safe paths from the order's castle inside Davokar to the nearest barbarian settlement, and since they spend much time patrolling the area they know about the geography close to the castle.

Of course, rumors claim that the high masters among the staff mages know much more than that, such as the precise location of, and secure routs to, the city of Symbar. But since they are unwilling to share such insights, they apparently believe that some knowledge can be dangerous.

Among staff mages in general, it is more or less obvious that there sooner or later will come a day when the Staff Masters will lead the order to Symbar, to reclaim the Throne of Thorns in a last, deciding battle against the powers of darkness.

in the air. Carved runes of a more permanent type are also made, but then usually in places where they are expected to remain over long periods of time and be "recharged" after having been activated. *Symbolism* includes the powers *Protective Runes, Draining Glyph, Blinding Symbol* and *Banishing Seal*.

RITUALS

As part of a tradition based on writing, symbolists have also put great emphasis on rituals, and the tradition teaches a series of unique rituals involving charged symbols and signs. They are primarily renowned for their tattoos and many older symbolists are covered with powerful rune tattoos, just as they offer the same type of protection and aid to their close allies.

Symbolism includes the rituals *Faraway Writing, Spell Trap, Carve Rune Tattoo* and *Rune Guardian*.

CORRUPTION

The origin of Symbolism can be traced back to the destruction of the east, and many rune crafters explain the birth of their tradition as based on the aim to resist and/or avoid corruption. As the east was drained of life and became the ruined, deserted wasteland it is today, the symbolists were busy advancing their knowledge. Not until the empire beyond the Ravens fell and the surrounding region proved to be devastated – the work of other mystics, according to symbolist legends – did the founding mystics of Symbolism flee across the mountains to the uninhabited river landscape that is today known as Vojvodar.

The strength of Symbolism is its resilience to corruption: symbolists do not suffer permanent corruption from learning the tradition's powers or from crafting symbols. They suffer some corruption when a symbol is activated, but less than the members of other traditions – only one point in temporary corruption per activated symbol. Symbolism's weakness is that it is slow; a symbolist trades his protection from corruption for the time it takes to craft the symbols. However, the rituals of *Symbolism* function just like the rituals of other traditions.

Staff Magic

THE ORDER OF Staff Magic consists of a number of ascetic warrior monks who see themselves as descendants to the guard of Symbaroum's last emperor. The staff mages live in their castle deep inside the forest, in the wild parts of Davokar where ruins from the fallen empire constantly remind them of their past failure. According to their myths, the fall of Symbaroum was directly connected to the death of the emperor, and as his bodyguards it was their duty to keep him alive. Hence, in the minds of the staff mages, the fall of Symbaroum was their doing and with the destruction of the empire, darkness entered this part of the world.

It is up to the now living staff mages to correct the errors of the past, meaning that they must fight corruption and finally resurrect the fallen empire. In the fight against corruption, they have a valuable ally in the Iron Pact; even if the mages are not official members of the pact, they often cooperate with the elves. However, the Iron Pact and the staff mages are not always in agreement, particularly on the idea that a new emperor must take his (or her) place on the Throne of Thorns – while the mages regard the emperor's death as the triggering factor, the elves remember the emperor himself as the root of all evil.

Aside from attacking those who from ignorance or a hunger for power fraternize with the powers of corruption, the staff mages continuously seek *"The descendant and rightful heir of the last emperor"*. The search is as difficult as it is frustrating, with many mages in serious disagreement regarding both how to orchestrate the search and who to define as the target. Most staff mages prefer the more tangible combat against abominations, sorcerers and the few treasure hunters who venture so far into Davokar that they get close to the heart of Symbaroum: the ruined city of Symbar and its empty throne.

THE TITLES OF STAFF MAGIC

The order of staff mages has three titles: Staffless (apprentices; i.e. established mystics who train with the order but have yet to earn a staff), Rune Staff (those who have received a staff) and finally the Staff Masters.

POWERS

The powers of *Staff Magic* are associated with the staff, seen as an extension of a true warrior mage's soul and as their foremost weapon. Adding to that, the tradition features a number of defensive powers that emanate from the runes on a staff.

Staff Magic includes the powers *Anathema, Protective Runes, Dancing Weapon, Sphere* and *Staff Projectile*.

RITUALS

Less experienced mages are usually not focused on learning rituals, but as soon as they establish themselves as skilled staff warriors they are quick to learn at least one of the tradition's offensive rituals: *Blood Storm* or *Quake*. In fact, it is expected by high ranking mages that they are able to unleash such destructive powers in combat, and Staff Masters always learn both of these and some rituals borrowed from other traditions.

The rituals of *Staff Magic* are performed in a special way: they are woven over the rune staff and then stored in it – with the staff vibrating from the force – until the mage thrusts it into the ground and utters a power word (requires a combat action). Then the power of the ritual takes effect.

Once a ritual has been stored, the staff cannot be used for other powers or rituals; if so, the stored ritual is abolished. However, the mage is free to activate the elemental runes of the staff (see the ability *Staff Magic*) and use it as a melee weapon, even with the powers of a ritual in store.

If a staff mage uses rituals from other traditions they work just like they normally would.

CORRUPTION

The order teaches that corruption is a side-effect of the negligent exercise of power. Mages do not regard corruption as immoral in itself, but emphasize that the corruption of the mystic can become the enemy's weapon; all mages are taught that sorcerers can use the mage's own corruption against him or her, which is why corruption must be avoided.

The order also keeps older and darker lessons alive, lessons that claim the careless use of mystical powers, rituals and artifacts not only affects the mystic who wields them, but also the surrounding world. As proof of this, they often refer to the deserted wasteland east of the Ravens – which at one time was flourishing farmlands and the cradle of humankind's first empire. And since the order, according to the mages, stems from the east, it is not unlikely that their moral tales on the importance of mystical restraint contain some grains of truth.

Troll Singing

AS A TRADITION, *Troll Singing* is as old as the race of trolls – at least, their collective memory remembers nothing before the songs. According to the myth, the troll race was created through the songs of the world, hummed by the spirits of air and dust, in rhythm with the tail of the World Serpent drumming against the bedrock.

To trolls, the songs of the skalds together with the hammering of the smiths, and the warriors' clawing at the stone walls of the Abyss compose the great hymn of life. The troll culture, the race, yes even the existence of single trolls, is unthinkable without the songs.

THE TITLES OF TROLL SINGING

Troll singers have no titles, but follow a simple apprenticeship system where a promising singer learns from a master. When an apprentice has learned enough they are tasked with serving the rulers as best they can, and later on the time comes to pass knowledge and skills on to some new apprentice.

POWERS

The powers of *Troll Singing* influence minds more than bodies, and often affect many listeners at a time, rather than a single target. Also, some of the powers are performed as hymns which can be sung in parallel with other activities – a combat hymn sung in battle may not be as powerful as other powers, but in combination with the blows of the hammer the effect is considerable.

Troll Singing includes the powers *Dancing Weapon, Weakening Hymn, Confusion, Heroic Hymn, Battle Hymn* and *Retribution*.

RITUALS

Troll Singing has few of its own rituals and those that exist are often about mending the broken or finding the lost, as in the rituals *Restore* and *Retrieve*. However, the lack of rituals within *Troll Singing* does not stop the skalds from learning rituals from other traditions.

CORRUPTION

To willingly accept corruption is unthinkable to most troll singers. Through the songs, the trolls remember the world as it was before the corruption, long before humans arrived and started building their empires. When Symbaroum grew dark from hunger and rapacity, the trolls welcomed the Elven intervention; they supported the Iron Pact and contributed to the birth of Davokar. At least this is said in the songs.

Nowadays, the trolls live beneath the woods in the Abyss where darkness broods; in cavities and caves it gathers in pools of malice. These birthplaces of abominations remind all trolls, singer or not, that the twilight or winter of the world has come. They also know that this twilight cannot be expelled by the eerie lights glowing in their underground halls; that this is a winter during which the even temperatures of the Underworld will not protect them from being bitten by the frost.

Powers and Rituals

IN THIS SECTION you will find the powers and rituals that the *Advanced Player's Guide* adds to the game. Note that some of them are exclusively meant for mystical professions, and hence not available for those who do not meet the profession's requirements. These powers are marked with the phrase "Only available to..." For instance, the power *Staff Projectile* is only available to staff mages, while the power *Sphere* belongs to *Staff Magic* but may be acquired by others.

BANISHING SEAL

Tradition: Symbolism
Material: A symbol created for the purpose

The mystic binds banishing energies to a symbol, that when unleashed sweeps out in waves over the area. Upon creation, the mystic must choose what type of creature will be affected (Abominations, Beasts, Cultural Beings or Undead).

Novice	**Active.** The symbol triggers a chain of banishing energies. The target closest to the symbol is affected if the mystic passes a *[Resolute←Resolute]* test; if this succeeds, an attempt is made to banish the next enemy and so on, until a test fails. Banished creatures must leave the area as quickly as they can and may not return before the end of the scene.
Adept	**Active.** Same as the novice level, but creatures that are unaffected (the test fails) suffer 1D4 damage from the power, ignoring Armor. Targets that are unaffected by the banishing effect can choose to flee to avoid being damaged; if so, they may not return until after the scene.
Master	**Active.** Same as the novice level, but those that are not banished suffer 1D8 damage, ignoring Armor. Targets that are unaffected by the banishing effect can choose to flee instead and only suffer 1D4 damage, ignoring Armor; if so, they may not return until after the scene.

Table 4: Mystical Powers

POWER	TRADITION	TRADITION	TRADITION
Anathema	Wizardry, Staff Magic, Theurgy	Maltransformation	Witchcraft
Banishing Seal	Symbolism	Mind-throw	Wizardry
Bend Will	Witchcraft, Wizardry, Sorcery	Mirroring	**Illusionist only**
Black Bolt	Sorcery	Nature's Embrace	Witchcraft
Black Breath	Sorcery	Prios' Burning Glass	Theurgy
Blessed Shield	Theurgy	Protective Runes	Staff Magic, Symbolism
Blinding Symbol	Symbolism	Psychic Thrust	**Mentalism only**
Brimstone Cascade	Wizardry	Purgatory	**Inquisitor only**
Combat Hymn	Troll Singing	Retribution	Sorcery, Troll Singing
Confusion	Wizardry, Troll Singing	Revenant Strike	Sorcery
Curse	Witchcraft, Sorcery	Shapeshift	Witchcraft
Dancing Weapon	Staff Magic, Troll Singing	Sphere	Staff Magic
Draining Glyph	Symbolism	Spirit Walk	**Necromancer only**
Entangling Vines	Witchcraft	Staff Projectile	**Staff Magic only**
Exorcize	**Demonologist only**	Storm Arrow	Witchcraft
Fire Soul	**Pyromancer only**	Teleport	**Demonologist only**
Flame Wall	Wizardry	Thorn Cloak	**Green Weaver only**
Heroic Hymn	Troll Singing	Tormenting Spirits	**Spiritualist & Necromancer only**
Holy Aura	Theurgy	True Form	Wizardry, Theurgy
Illusory Correction	Wizardry	Unholy Aura	Sorcery
Inherit Wound	Witchcraft, Theurgy	Unnoticeable	Wizardry, Theurgy
Larvae Boils	Witchcraft, Sorcery	Weakening Hymn	Troll Singing
Lay on Hands	Witchcraft, Theurgy	Wild Hunt	**Blood Wader only**
Levitate	Wizardry, Theurgy	Witch Hammer	Theurgy
Lifegiver	**Confessor only**		

BLACK BOLT

Tradition: Sorcery
Material: A shard of volcanic glass

During The Great War, the black bolts of the Dark Lords, ensnaring and burning their targets, were feared by all. In more recent days, other sorcerers have discovered that they can do the same, by extending their tainted souls and using them as a whip that traps and corrodes the enemy.

The mystic cannot cast a new black bolt as long as at least one enemy is ensnared by the power, but he or she is free to make use of other mystical powers.

Novice	**Active.** With a passed *[Resolute←Quick]* test, the character casts a black bolt at an enemy. If successful, the target is hit and suffers 1D6 damage, ignoring *Armor*. Also, the target is trapped and may not act until it manages to break free, which requires a passed *Resolute* test (one roll is made each turn after the first) or happens automatically if the mystic loses concentration, *[Resolute –Damage]*.
Adept	**Active.** The character casts a chain of black bolts. This works just like at the novice level, but for every target that is hit by the bolt another enemy may be attacked, until a failed success test is rolled. All affected enemies may try to break free from the effect of the power, and if one of them succeeds all of them are immediately free to act. The same happens if the mystic loses concentration, *[Resolute –Damage]*.
Master	**Active.** The character casts a chain of black bolts, just like at the adept level, but ensnared targets must break free individually; they cannot help each other like at the adept level. If the mystic loses concentration *[Resolute –Damage]* all targets are immediately freed from the entangling darkness.

BLACK BREATH

Tradition: Sorcery
Material: The mystic's own permanent corruption.

A mystic with permanent corruption can spew out its inner darkness and infect others with corruption, or heal already tainted creatures.

Novice	**Active.** One (1) creature is hit; roll 1D4 against its total corruption. If the roll is equal to or lower than the corruption value, the creature heals an amount equal to the outcome of the roll; if higher, the creature suffers the outcome in temporary corruption.
Adept	**Active.** Like Novice, but the roll is 1D6.

Master	**Active.** Same as Adept level, but the attack is made in a chain, where another target is hit if the previous one suffered corruption. As soon as someone is healed, the chain is broken.

BLINDING SYMBOL

Tradition: Symbolism
Material: A prepared symbol

Intricate runes emit energies that can temporarily blind those who are bedazzled by the light. The effect of a *Blinding Symbol* is immediately suspended if the victim uses a dose of Eye Drops.

Novice	**Active.** The runes trigger a chain of blinding energies. The target closest to the symbol is blinded if the mystic passes a *[Resolute←Resolute]* test; if this succeeds, an attempt is made to blind the next enemy and so on, until a test fails. The victims are only blinded for one turn before automatically regaining their sight.
Adept	**Active.** Same effect as the novice level. However, the effect lasts until the mystic fails a *Resolute* test or loses concentration *[Resolute –Damage]*.
Master	**Active.** Same effect as the novice level. However, the effect lasts until the afflicted regains *Toughness* from healing powers or elixirs.

COMBAT HYMN

Tradition: Troll Singing
Material: None, but the mystic must sing out loud

There is a raw and untamed power in singing, and some mystics learn to sing while fighting to gain considerable extra strength when battling the enemy. The character is one of those who have learned to sing combat hymns to increase his or her chances in combat. The song is interrupted if the mystic uses another mystical power or if concentration is lost due to taking damage *[Resolute –Damage]*.

Novice	**Free.** The character gives himself and all allies a +1 bonus to either *Quick*, *Strong* or *Accurate* (the ally chooses what attribute will be affected) for as long as the singing continues.
Adept	**Free.** The character gives himself and all allies a +1 bonus to *Quick*, *Strong* and *Accurate* for as long as the singing continues.
Master	**Free.** The character and all allies gain a +1 bonus to *Quick*, *Strong* and *Accurate* for as long as the singing continues. Also, the character and all allies regain 1D6 *Toughness* when the song begins; this healing effect may only be used once per scene.

DANCING WEAPON

Tradition: Staff Magic, Troll Singing
Material: A melee weapon

By willpower alone, the mystic makes a weapon soar and fight, with the speed and agility of a thought.

The weapon in question does not have to be special in any way; if it has qualities or powers, these may be used by the mystic according to standard rules of combat. However, the mystic cannot use other abilities related to melee combat while using this power.

Novice   **Active.** The mystic lets a weapon dance and uses *Resolute* instead of both *Accurate* (attack) and *Quick* (defense). Other than that, normal combat rules apply.

      The novice must focus on the weapon while fighting, which prevents him or her from using other powers or abilities while the weapon dances.

Adept   **Active.** The mystic must take control of the weapon by spending a combat action to activate the power, but then the weapon fights on its own while the mystic is free to use other powers and abilities. Both attack and defense rolls are made against *Resolute*.

Master   **Free.** The weapon dances out of the scabbard when the master needs it, attacks once per turn and defends the character by itself, leaving the mystic free to use other powers and abilities. Both attack and defense rolls are made against *Resolute*.

DRAINING GLYPH

Tradition: Symbolism
Material: A carefully crafted glyph

The mystic creates a glyph that upon activation becomes a whirling vortex, sucking the life-force from the enemy. The glyph affects all enemies who can see the symbol and are in front of it.

Novice   **Active.** With a *[Resolute←Strong]* test the mystic can damage every enemy in the vicinity (one test per target). The damage is 1D4, ignoring Armor. The effect lasts until the mystic fails a *Resolute* test or loses concentration *[Resolute −Damage]*.

Adept   **Active.** Same as the novice level, but the effect lasts until the mystic fails a *Resolute* test.

Master   **Active.** The master can direct part of the drained energy into himself or his allies; the stolen life-force heals the mystic or one of its allies, returning 1D4 points of *Toughness* per turn for as long as effect is active.

EXORCIZE

Tradition: Only available to Demonologists
Material: A sharp weapon to cut the world's fabric

A Sorcerer's lack of respect for the laws of nature lends him or her the astounding ability to tear at and bend apparent constants like time and space. One way to make use of this is to temporarily banish creatures from the world of the living, out into the Yonderworld where alien winds howl in chorus with hunting abominations.

This poses a danger for the demonologist, since every failed attempt to use the power risks bringing an abomination into the world. If this happens, the abomination attacks a random victim, though not someone who is protected by an *Unholy Aura* or whose soul is already thoroughly corrupt.

The abomination that comes has an equal chance (1D6) of being (1-2) a Vindictive Daemon, 3-4) a Knowledgeable Daemon, or (5-6) a Guardian Daemon (for stats, see the ritual *Summon Daemon* on page 94).

Novice   **Active.** With a successful *[Resolute←Resolute]* test, the character opens a temporary rift in the world's fabric and sends an enemy through it. The enemy returns one turn later, on the characters initiative and in the same location – steaming from the mists of the Yonderworld and having suffered 1D4 Damage (ignoring Armor) and 1D4 temporary corruption.

      A failed attempt automatically attracts an abomination that enters through the rift.

Adept   **Active.** With a successful test against *[Resolute←Resolute]*, the character sends an enemy further out into the Yonderworld and he or she must struggle to get back; each turn the enemy may roll a *Resolute* test, a success brings it back to the world. Every turn spent in the Yonderworld deals 1D4 damage (ignoring Armor) and 1D4 temporary corruption. If the target dies or becomes blight-born, the rift closes and the enemy is gone for good.

      Since the rift is open for as long as the enemy is expelled, there is a risk that a wrathful abomination slips through – every turn after the first, the mystic must pass a *Resolute* test to stop an abomination from entering through the rift.

      If the initial test for using the power fails, the mystic must immediately roll a *Resolute* test to stop a raging abomination from slipping through into the world.

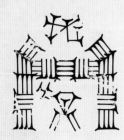

Cuneiform scribblings found on a castle ruin northwest of Karvosti; probably a more recent forgery, carved by a barbarian or possibly even an Ambrian.

The mystic may choose not to try and stop the abomination from entering, no matter if the abomination comes as an effect of a failed attempt to use the power or as a consequence of a successful long-lasting rift.

Master	**Reaction.** Once per turn, one enemy that attacks the mystic in melee is at risk of being expelled to the Yonderworld, *[Resolute←Resolute]*. If expelled, he or she suffers the same effect as at the novice level. A failed test has no effect; there is no risk that an abomination enters into the world.

FIRE SOUL

Tradition: Only available to Pyromancers
Material: None, but Fire Souls often display physical signs of their attraction to fire; a burning gaze, red hair or heat that radiates from the body.

Pyromancers have found that those who dedicate their lives to the study of fire in time learn to instinctively use it as a shield and a weapon. It is even said that the most devoted learn to manipulate the force of hostile fires and paradoxically enough use these burning powers to heal themselves when wounded.

Novice	**Reaction.** When the mystic is hit in melee combat, flames strike out at the attacker, dealing 1D6 damage. Also, the mystic suffers less damage from fire, meaning that he or she has +1D6 Armor to damage from that element.
Adept	**Reaction.** Like the novice level, except the protection from fire and the damage dealt against those attacking the mystic in melee combat are rolled with 1D10 instead of 1D6.
Master	**Reaction.** The master's power is so great that he or she does not take damage but is instead healed by fire. The mystic recovers half of any damage that would have been dealt by fire (if the mystic should have suffered 4 damage, he or she instead heals 2 *Toughness*). This also pertains to fire created by the mystic when using other powers besides Fire Soul.

In addition, the flames that lash out from the mystic when he or she is attacked now also retaliate at range. Powers that affect the mind will not trigger such a retaliation, but powers which potentially deal damage do. The striking flames deal 1D10 damage and Armor protects as usual. |

HEROIC HYMN

Tradition: Troll Singing
Material: None, but the mystic must sing out loud
There is power in the heroic hymns of old. The mystic can sing while fighting, thereby filling his or her allies with courage and vigor.

The song is interrupted if the mystic uses another mystical power or if concentration is lost by taking damage *[Resolute –Damage]*.

Novice	**Free.** The character gives himself and all allies a +1 bonus to either *Cunning*, *Resolute* or *Persuasive* (the ally chooses what attribute will be affected) for as long as the singing continues.
Adept	**Free.** The character gives himself and all allies a +1 bonus to *Cunning*, *Resolute* and *Persuasive* for as long as the singing continues.
Master	**Free.** The character and all allies gain a +1 bonus to *Cunning*, *Resolute* and *Persuasive* for as long as the singing continues. Also, the temporary corruption of the character and all allies is reduced by 1D4 when the song begins; this corruption reducing effect may only be used once per scene.

LIFEGIVER

Tradition: Only available to Confessors
Material: A drop of pure water
The wellspring of life runs clear and refreshing in these dark days. Dedicated healers can draw from its power and transform it into a purifying gift that cleanses souls of corruption and heals physical wounds.

Novice	**Active.** The mystic washes away 1D4 points of temporary corruption from a creature in sight. Any excess points heal the creature's *Toughness* instead. The mystic may use this power on him- or herself.
Adept	**Active.** The mystic washes away 1D4 points of temporary corruption from himself and all allies in sight. Any excess points heal *Toughness* instead.
Master	**Reaction.** The mere presence of the Confessor directly reduces the harmful effect of temporary corruption on all allies in sight. When an ally uses a mystical power or an artifact that gives corruption, the amount suffered is reduced by 1D4 points. Any excess points have no effect.

In this case, the power has no effect on the mystic using it; the player character suffers from temporary corruption when using powers and artifacts as usual. |

MIRRORING

Tradition: Only available to Illusionist
Material: A couple of small figurines

Reality's layers of misconceptions and lies may be used to project a series of conceivable phenomena, only one of which corresponds to the reality of the world. The multiple false images created this way serve to protect the mystic from hostile attacks – in most cases; there is always the risk that the enemy targets the mystic instead of an illusion. Every attack against the mystic has a chance of hitting one of the projections or the mystic: if three illusions are made, the chance of the mystic being targeted is 1 out of 4. As the illusions are destroyed, the mystic's risk of being hit increases.

Novice   **Active.** With a passed *Resolute* test, the mystic projects 1D4 mirror copies of himself. If a copy is hit, it ceases to exist. Damage from area effects hit the mystic as usual and instantaneously dispel all mirror copies.

Adept   **Active.** With a passed *Resolute* test, the mystic projects 1D6 mirror copies of himself. Damage from area effects hit the mystic as usual and dispel one mirror copy.

Master   **Active.** With a passed *Resolute* test, the mystic projects 1D8 mirror copies of himself. Damage from area effects hit the mystic as usual but dispel no mirror copies.

PROTECTIVE RUNES

Tradition: Staff Magic, Symbolism
Material: A depiction of the runes

The mystic's runes emit protective energies that surround the mystic and at higher levels also punish his or her enemies.

Novice   **Active.** The power of the runes offers +1D4 to Armor until the mystic fails a *Resolute* test or loses concentration *[Resolute – Damage]*. The extra die of Armor is rolled separately with each hit and is added to any other Armor.

Adept   **Active.** The runes provide +1D4 to Armor (see the novice level). A retaliating effect also inflicts 1D4 damage on every enemy that harms the protected creature, ignoring any Armor. The effect lasts until the mystic fails a *Resolute* test or loses concentration *[Resolute –Damage]*.

Master   **Active.** The protective and retaliating effects are rolled with 1D6 instead of 1D4, and it lasts until the mystic fails a *Resolute* test.

PSYCHIC THRUST

Tradition: Only available to Mentalists
Material: A shard of glass, sharp as a knife

Some mystics know how to project their will to form a psychic weapon that can attack the enemy together with the mystic's ordinary melee attacks. This means that the enemy must defend on two fronts, and risk failing at both. There is also a chance that the enemy will be paralyzed or severely damaged by the psychic thrust.

Novice   **Reaction.** The mystic performs a normal melee attack in combination with a psychic thrust, aimed at the enemy's defensive capability. The character gains a second chance to succeed on the attack test.

Adept   **Reaction.** The psychic thrust is made in combination with the melee attack, and if the mystic passes a *[Resolute←Resolute]* test the enemy is incapable of defending against the attack. Hence, if this test is successful, the mystic automatically hits the enemy.

Master   **Reaction.** With a successful test against *[Resolute←Resolute]* the enemy is unable to defend and the melee attack hits automatically. Moreover, the enemy suffers 1D4 extra damage, ignoring Armor, in addition to the damage dealt by the melee attack.

PURGATORY

Tradition: Only available to Inquisitors
Material: A short piece of a rusty chain

Blackened souls echo with pain and darkness, and a trained Inquisitor can use that darkness against the enemy, or even drown the twisted target in its own inner blackness.

Novice   **Active.** The mystic forces one target to roll 1D20 against its total corruption. An outcome equal to or lower leads to acute pain that incapacitates the target for a whole turn. Thoroughly corrupt creatures automatically suffer 1D6 damage instead, ignoring armor.

Adept   **Active.** The mystic forces all enemies in sight to roll 1D20 against their total corruption. An outcome equal to or lower leads to acute pain that incapacitates the target for a whole turn. Thoroughly corrupt creatures automatically suffer 1D6 damage instead, ignoring armor.

Novice   **Reaction.** The mystic automatically punishes all enemies in sight who happen to attract corruption. The mystic may exclude any allies from the effect.

Each point in corruption suffered through the use of powers or artifacts deals the same amount of physical damage to the enemy, ignoring Armor.

RETRIBUTION

Tradition: Sorcery, Troll Singing
Material: None, only harmful words

Some dark-minded mystics can use their anger and vindictiveness to amass dark energies around a creature they want to hurt. In fact, at the higher levels the effect of this ability becomes instinctive, and all pain that the mystic suffers will undoubtedly be transferred to any enemies in the vicinity.

Note that members of the race Dwarf can learn *Retribution* as if it was a normal ability. Hence, they suffer no corruption from using this particular power, neither when they learn it, nor when they make use of it. This pertains only to this power and the dwarven race.

Novice	**Active.** If the character utters words of doom and passes a *[Resolute←Resolute]* test, misfortune gathers in a dense cloud around an enemy. All who attack the target get a second chance to pass their attack tests during the rest of the scene. Only one enemy at a time can suffer the mystic's Retribution this way; changing the target counts as a combat action.
Adept	**Reaction.** When the character suffers damage and passes a *[Resolute←Resolute]* test, the attacker is bound by a death link. Only one enemy at a time can be bound by a death link, but if a link is broken a new enemy who damages the character can be bound.

The death link means that damage suffered by the character is also inflicted upon the bound enemy. This includes all damage, irrespective of source.

The *Pain Threshold* is not affected; it is handled separately for the character and the target. Attacks that do not deal damage can be ignored, but in the case of powers that deal damage as part of their effect, any and all damage is transferred through the link. Damage from the monstrous trait Alternative Damage is also transferred to the target.

If the character dies (becomes dead or dying) the link is immediately broken and the damage from the attack that felled the character is not transferred. |
| Master | **Reaction.** Same as at the adept level, but each time the character suffers damage |

from an attack and passes a *[Resolute←Resolute]* test, the attacker is bound by a death link. Hence, the number of creatures bound is unlimited.

SPHERE

Tradition: Staff Magic
Material: Rune staff or melee weapon

The mystic has his or her staff – or another melee weapon – spin around at such velocity that it forms a protective sphere. The sphere effectively parries most attacks. On the negative side, the mystic cannot perform attacks or use other powers without dispelling the sphere. The sphere is active until it is willingly aborted, until the mystic uses another power or until it is dispelled by some other mystic using the power *Anathema*.

Novice	**Active.** The sphere lets the mystic choose to defend using *Resolute* instead of *Quick*. It can protect the mystic from melee and ranged attacks but not from mystical powers. Only movement is allowed while within the sphere – not even actions which normally can replace movement are possible while maintaining the sphere.
Adept	**Active.** The sphere automatically defends against an unlimited number of melee and ranged attacks as long as it is active. However, it does not provide any protection against mystical powers and area effects like explosions, smoke bombs or similar.
Master	**Active.** The master can make a weapon form a sphere without having to touch it. That way, he or she may include an ally inside the sphere. Also, this leaves the hands of the mystic free for other actions, such as drinking an elixir, bandage an ally's wounds or unrolling a spell scroll – i.e. such actions that can replace a movement action. The mystic cannot affect the world outside the sphere, but can maintain mystical effects which are already active – the same goes for any ally the mystic protects inside the sphere.

SPIRIT WALK

Tradition: Only available to Necromancers
Material: A piece of a burial gown

Because of his or her closeness to death, the mystic has developed the mystical skill to assume the immaterial form of a spirit. *Spirit Walk* is hindered by *Magic Circle*, *Witch Circle* and *Sanctifying Rite*; the mystic cannot pass through or leave such areas while moving in the form of a spirit; however, it

is possible to assume the spirit form when inside such protected domains. The *Spirit Walk* also ends if someone lights a Ghost Candle close by (see the alchemical elixir with that name, on page 153 in the *Core Rulebook*).

Novice	**Whole Turn.** With a passed *Resolute* test, the mystic assumes spirit form. This immaterial form lasts for one movement action (about 10 meters), making it possible to move through even the thickest walls, or, for that matter, through enemies on the battlefield. All attacks aimed at the mystic are ignored unless they are made with mystical powers or artifacts – both deal only half damage. The movement is all that the character can do during the turn, and after having moved he or she reassumes his or her physical form.
Adept	**Reaction.** The spirit form comes instinctively to the mystic. When attacked the mystic may roll [*Resolute –Damage*] instead of a *Defense* test; if successful the attack passes

through the mystic without dealing damage. The exceptions are mystical powers and artifacts, which deal half damage even if the test is passed. The mystic immediately returns to its physical form.

The mystic can choose to roll *Defense* as usual if he or she prefers, i.e. not use Spirit Walk to avoid a specific attack.

Master	**Reaction.** With a passed *Resolute* test, the mystic can let an attack – from a weapon or a mystical power dealing damage – start in spirit form and then transcend into physical form once the enemy's armor has been penetrated; if so, the Armor of the target is ignored by the mystic's attack.

STAFF PROJECTILE

Tradition: Only available to Staff Mages
Material: A rune staff

In the hands of a staff mage, the rune staff is a powerful throwing weapon. The staff is thrown at an enemy and returns to the mystic's hand, whether it hits or not.

View over the northern reaches of the Black Pitch Mire and some of the stone statues standing in the marshland. That they are composed of stone is known, but not if they were created that way…

Novice	**Active.** The mystic throws the staff and may roll against *Resolute* instead of *Accurate* to hit the target. The staff deals 1D8 damage; the effect of a possibly activated elemental rune (see Staff Magic) is added.
Adept	**Active.** Like novice, but the projectile deals 1D10 damage. The staff may be thrown past blocking terrain or enemies to reach a target further away; the mystic does not need a clear line of sight but has to see at least part of the target. The effect of a possibly activated elemental rune (see Staff Magic) is added.
Master	**Active.** The staff is thrown in a chain and the mystic may use *Resolute* instead of *Accurate* to hit. The first hit deals 1D12, the second 1D10, the third 1D8, the forth 1D6 and the fifth 1D4. The chain is not broken by missing an attack test, but the damage is reduced with each target, hit or no hit. More than five targets cannot be targeted by the Staff Projectile; the mystic must see the target but does not need a clear line of sight. The effect of a possibly activated elemental rune (see Staff Magic) is added.

TELEPORT

Tradition: Only available to Demonologist
Material: A sharp weapon to cut the world's fabric

The sorcerers who have gone furthest in questioning the laws of nature can tear holes in the world and step outside, only to tear another rift in the fabric of the Yonderworld and reenter the world of the living in a new location. As always when the shell of reality is perforated, there is a risk that an abomination slips through and attacks a random creature – except those protected by the power *Unholy Aura* or whose souls are thoroughly corrupt.

The abomination that comes has an equal chance (1D6) of being (1–2) a Vindictive Daemon, 3–4) a Knowledgeable Daemon, or (5–6) a Guardian Daemon (for stats, see the ritual *Summon Daemon* on page 94).

How Much do You See of the Yonderworld?

The creature who, willingly or not, is thrown into the Yonderworld finds itself in a flowing wasteland. The ground is covered in ashes and even the air is full of whirling soot flakes that feel glowing hot against the skin. If unlucky, the creature lands in the lap of some daemonic abomination; otherwise, such beings can be seen in the distance or heard howling from hunger.

Novice	**Active.** With a passed *Resolute* test, the character can exit the world and return within a range of two movement actions. The mystic suffers 1D4 damage from the journey through the Yonderworld, ignoring Armor. The teleportation does not trigger a Free Attack, even if withdrawing from melee. The mystic must see the return location when the mystical power is activated. If the test fails an enraged daemon enters through the rift instead.
Adept	**Active.** Same as at the novice level, except the mystic suffers no damage during his or her trip to the Yonderworld. If the test fails, the mystic must pass a *Resolute* test to stop an enraged abomination from entering through the rift in the world. The mystic can choose not to stop the entry and willingly let the daemon get through.
Master	**Active.** Same as at the Adept level, with the addition that the mystic may take someone along on the journey. This someone must stand next to the mystic when the power is activated (melee range) and if the creature is reluctant, the mystic must pass a *[Resolute←Resolute]* test to force it to follow. The fellow traveler suffers 1D4 damage, ignoring Armor, and also 1D4 temporary corruption from the traumatic experience. If the test fails, the mystic must pass a *Resolute* test to stop an enraged abomination from entering through the rift in the world. The mystic can choose not to stop the entry and willingly let the daemon get through.

THORN CLOAK

Tradition: Only available to Green Weavers
Material: A thorn bush branch

The plants in nature are usually seen as still and reactive rather than aggressive and active. Experienced green weavers know better and can use surrounding vines, thorns and roots to defend themselves and their allies.

| Novice | **Active.** The mystic allows himself to be entwined by vegetation, which provides a bonus of +1D4 in Armor, or +1D6 if the mystic does not move during the whole turn. |
| Adept | **Active.** Same as at the novice level, but the vegetation branches out to also protect any allies who stand close to the mystic (inside melee range). These allies gain a +1D4 |

bonus to Armor, but this extra protection disappears if they move away from the mystic, or if the mystic moves away from the allies.

Master **Active.** The mystic and its allies are protected as at the adept level, with the addition that the vegetation strikes back at enemy attackers. Every successful hit in melee against the mystic or a protected ally inflicts 1D10 damage (ignoring Armor) upon the attacker due to lashing thorns.

TORMENTING SPIRITS

Tradition: Only available to Spiritualists and Necromancers

Material: A piece of a burial gown

The world is old and many spirits linger from days past; nature spirits in dirt and water, or dead heroes who are yet to pass over to the other side. Some mystics can wake spirits to life and make them attack their enemies. The enemies are beset with these fiery spirits who tear at their clothes, equipment, hair and flesh. At best, the target cannot act; at worst, the target is driven mad or even dies from the attacks.

Novice **Active.** The mystic calls spirits to his or her aid, and these transparent shapes attack an enemy. The target automatically fails all tests for concentration while using mystical powers; all other tests have a second chance to fail. The mystic must pass a *Resolute* test each turn in order for the spirits to continue their attacks.

Adept **Active.** The mystic may demand more substantial help from the spirits. They attack ferociously and deal damage to *Resolute*, adding to the effect described at the novice level. The damage dealt is 1D4 per turn, ignoring armor. If *Resolute* is reduced to zero the target dies, presuming they are not allowed to roll death tests (like characters). The latter instead becomes temporarily insane – catatonic, crying or otherwise unable to act – while rolling their death tests. The *Resolute* damage heals like other damages. The mystic must pass a *Resolute* test each turn in order for the spirits to continue their attack. Also, if the mystic takes damage, concentration will be broken if failing a [*Resolute –Damage*] test.

Master **Active.** Like adept, but the spirit attacks deal 1D6 damage to *Resolute*.

WEAKENING HYMN

Tradition: Troll Singing

Material: None, but the mystic must sing out loud

Throughout history, many taunting songs have been written about the faint of heart and in these tunes there are debilitating harmonies to be exploited by mystics who know how. The mystic repeatedly sings this infectious theme while fighting, thereby spreading cowardliness and weakness amongst his or her enemies.

The song is interrupted if the mystic uses another mystical power or if concentration is lost by taking damage [*Resolute –Damage*].

Novice **Free.** With a passed [*Persuasive←Resolute*] test, the mystic can give each wounded enemy a second chance to fail all success tests while the singing continues; one test is made for each wounded enemy.

Adept **Free.** With a passed [*Persuasive←Resolute*] test, the mystic can give each enemy (wounded or not) a second chance to fail all success tests while the singing continues.

Master **Free.** With a passed [*Persuasive←Resolute*] test, the mystic can give each enemy (wounded or not) a second chance to fail all success tests. Furthermore, all enemies that fail a success test because of the Weakening Hymn suffer 1D4 damage, ignoring armor – caused by them being physically affected by harrowing lyrics that conjure past failures.

WILD HUNT

Tradition: Only available to Blood Waders

Material: The fur of a beast dead from natural causes

Davokar's nature may seem dark and full of conflicts, trapped in an eternal cycle of birth, strife and death. But to mystics who have the capability to see the deeper truth, there is a perfect imbalance to this cycle; a higher form of harmony. This insight can be used by the mystic to acquire the help of seemingly hostile creatures of the Beast category.

The summoned beasts may not be of the same type as the enemies; otherwise the type is decided by which types occur naturally in the environment. The character dictates how the beasts act during the scene, after which they turn and leave the area.

Novice **Active.** The mystic can summon one weak beast to aid him or her in combat.

Adept **Active.** The mystic calls one ordinary beast or 1D4 weak beasts to aid him or her in combat.

Master **Active.** The mystic calls one challenging beast, 1D4 ordinary beasts or 1D6 weak beasts to aid him or her in combat.

Rituals

THIS SECTION INTRODUCES a series of new rituals, among these a number of Higher Rituals which are only available to the members of certain profession/specialization: they are not secret, but are impossible for others to perform since they require a special insight that none but the dedicated students of a particular area have.

Note that a character who belongs to a mystic profession must first acquire the base level ritual the normal way, before being able to choose it again and get it upgraded to the higher level.

ANOINT

Tradition: Theurgy

The mystic anoints him- or herself with holy oils before a battle, thereby gaining the following: +10 temporary *Toughness*, +1D4 in protection in addition to any *Armor* worn, and +1D4 damage on all attacks. If the mystic is damaged, he or she first loses the temporary *Toughness*, before his or her own *Toughness* is affected.

The downside is that the mystic cannot be healed and that all death tests automatically fail during the scene. The effect lasts for the duration of a scene.

ATONEMENT

Tradition: Only available to Confessors

The higher level of the ritual *Exorcism* makes the theurg able to lighten the spiritual burdens of a non-possessed person; this is done by the sinner accepting to perform a task for the Confessor. The task must be time-consuming and expensive or dangerous, usually some good deed for the Sun Church or for Prios in general. Once the task is accomplished, the sinner's permanent corruption is reduced by 1D4.

The ritual costs one point of *Experience* to perform, paid by the confessor or the sinner (the mystic decides).

BEAST COMPANION

Tradition: Only available to Blood Waders

The higher level of the ritual *Familiar* binds the beast to the mystic's body and soul; if the familiar dies it is resurrected at dawn the following morning. The mystic suffers damage when the familiar dies, as before. Should the beast companion become thoroughly corrupt – through the ritual *Blood Bond* or in some other way – the link between the mystic and the beast is forever broken.

BEWITCHING LANDSCAPE

Tradition: Wizardry

The mystic can weave a grand illusion over a location, making all who enter the area confused, lost and at risk of starving to death if they cannot break the spell.

The mystic enthralls every creature in the area with a passed [Resolute←Cunning] test; the victims gain a second chance to break the spell if one of their companions passes the test and then rolls a successful *Persuasive* test.

The effect can temporarily be dispelled with *Anathema*; otherwise it can only be permanently broken by the mystic who wove the illusion.

BLACK SYMPATHY

Tradition: Witchcraft, Sorcery, Theurgy

With a passed *Resolute* test, the mystic can inflict pain on an enemy from a distance, by damaging a doll or driving nails into a trace left by the target. The ritual also requires a mystical link to the victim – some hair strands, a puddle of blood or an item that the target holds dear.

The victim does not suffer any damage but experiences acute pains and cannot heal by any means during the days of torment. It takes the tormentor one hour to perform the ritual, but no success test is needed after the first. *Black Sympathy* can be aborted with the ritual *Break Link*. After that, the *Black Sympathy* cannot be resumed using the same mystical link, nor before thirty days have passed, even if a new link is available.

BLOOD STORM

Tradition: Only available to Staff Mages

The staff mage binds a storm of blood in the rune staff, to be unleashed with a thrust into the ground. The storm rages over the area, with the mystic standing in its calm eye. The mystic and allies standing nearby are unaffected, as are any enemies within melee range. All further out are hit by the full effect of the *Blood Storm*.

Those caught in the storm are blinded. Other than moving blindly, they must pass a *Vigilant* test each turn to be able to perform any actions. Even if they pass that test, they have a second chance to fail on all success tests.

The *Blood Storm* also has a drowning effect; it actively aims for the mouth and nose, and penetrates into the lungs, dealing 1D4 damage each turn, ignoring *Armor*. The only way to stop this is to leave the area, enter into close combat, flee to some place outside, or take refuge within a windowless structure.

The *Blood Storm* lasts until the mystic fails a *Resolute* test or loses concentration from being damaged, [Resolute –Damage].

Table 5: Rituals

RITUAL	TRADITION	RITUAL	TRADITION
Anoint	Theurgy	Magic Circle	Wizardry
Atonement	**Confessor only**	Nature's Lullaby	Witchcraft
Beast Companion	**Blood Wader only**	Necromancy	Witchcraft
Bewitching Landscape	Wizardry	Oracle	Theurgy
Black Sympathy	Witchcraft, Sorcery, Theurgy	Patron Saint	Theurgy
Blood Bond	Witchcraft	Phylactery	Sorcery
Blood Storm	**Staff Mage only**	Piercing Gaze	**Inquisitor only**
Borrow Beast	Witchcraft	Possess	Sorcery
Break Link	Wizardry	Purging Fire	Theurgy
Burdened by Fate	Witchcraft	Quake	**Staff Mage only**
Carve Rune Tattoo	Symbolist	Quick Growth	Witchcraft
Clairvoyance	Wizardry	Raise Undead	Sorcery
Command Confession	Theurgy	Restore	Troll Singing
Death Divination	**Spiritualist only**	Retrieve	Troll Singing
Death Lord	**Necromancer only**	Rune Guardian	Symbolism
Desecrating Rite	Sorcery	Sanctifying Rite	Theurgy
Enslave	Sorcery	Sanctum	Wizardry
Exchange Shadow	Sorcery	Sealing/Opening Rite	Troll Singing
Exorcism	Theurgy	Servant Daemon	**Demonologist only**
False Shape	Wizardry	Seven-league Stride	Wizardry
False Terrain	Wizardry	Soul Stone	Wizardry
Familiar	Witchcraft	Soul Trap	Sorcery
Faraway Writing	Symbolism	Spell Trap	Symbolism
Fata Morgana	Illusionist only	Spell Tunnel	**Mentalist only**
Flaming Servant	Wizardry	Summon Daemon	**Demonologist only**
Flesh Craft	Sorcery	Summoning	Witchcraft
Fortune-telling	Witchcraft	Tale of Ashes	Wizardry
Heretic's Trail	Theurgy	Telepathic Interrogation	Wizardry
Holy Smoke	Theurgy	Torment	Witchcraft
Illusion	Wizardry	Traceless	Witchcraft
Judging Bonds	Theurgy	Turn Weather	Witchcraft
Life Extension	Wizardry	Twin Servants	**Pyromancer only**
Living Fortress	**Green Weavers only**	Witch Circle	Witchcraft

The Higher Rituals

The following professions and corresponding higher rituals are known:

WITCHCRAFT:
Spiritualists:
Necromancy becomes *Death Divination*
Blood Wader:
Familiar becomes *Beast Companion*
Green Weaver:
Quick Growth becomes *Living Fortress*

WIZARDRY
Illusionist:
False Terrain becomes *Fata Morgana*
Mentalist:
Clairvoyance becomes *Spell Tunnel*
Pyromancer:
Flaming Servant becomes *Twin Servants*

SORCERY
Demonologist:
Summon Daemon becomes *Servant Daemon*
Necromancer:
Raise Undead becomes *Death Lord*

THEURGY
Inquisitor:
Holy Smoke becomes *Piercing Gaze*
Confessor:
Exorcism becomes *Atonement*

BURDENED BY FATE

Tradition: Witchcraft

With a passed *Resolute* test, the mystic binds a creature to a mission. The ritual requires a mystical link to the target – some hair strands, a puddle of blood or an item that the target holds dear. If successful, the target immediately knows what it must do but not who has actually bound him or her to the mission or task. The effect of the ritual is that the creature has a second chance to pass one test per scene while trying to complete the mission. On the other hand, he or she has a second chance to fail all tests during scenes which are not directly related to the mission.

Burdened by Fate can be dispelled by the ritual *Break Link*.

CARVE RUNE TATTOO

Tradition: Symbolism

The mystic carves power runes into the skin of a creature, giving the target the ability *Rune Tattoo*. The tattoo must then be paid for by "offering" 10 *Experience* or permanent corruption; it is possible to combine these, and pay part of the cost in *Experience* and the rest in corruption. The target can pay in full or the symbolist can contribute with the whole or a part of the cost.

DEATH DIVINATION

Tradition: Only available to Spiritualists

At the higher level of the ritual *Necromancy*, the mystic has a second chance to pass all tests to get answers from the spirits of the dead.

DEATH LORD

Tradition: Only available to Necromancers

The higher level of the ritual *Raise Undead* lets the necromancer summon an undead creature of greater power, a *Death Lord*; a blackened skeleton in soot-covered full plate armor, that performs the mystic's bidding with eyes that burn from behind the visor. Death Lords are smart and take their own initiative when solving problems; they often command hordes of lesser undead or act as the bodyguards of their makers.

The Death Lord is handled like a second character, and gains *Experience* and is developed just like a player character.

FALSE SHAPE

Tradition: Wizardry

The mystic weaves an illusory image around itself or an ally, who then assumes a different physical appearance. This cannot be the appearance of a specific individual, only of a typical version of the member of a race. The mystic can decide on form

DEATH LORD	
Race	Undead
Resistance	Ordinary
Traits	*Gravely Cold* (I), *Undead* (I)
Abilities	*Iron Fist* (novice), *Man-at-arms* (novice), *Two-handed Force* (novice)
Weapons	Heavy Weapon 1D12
Armor	Full Plate 1D10
Defense	7
Toughness	15 **Pain Threshold** –
Equipment	None
Shadow	Same as the master

Accurate 13 (−3), **Cunning** 10 (0), **Discreet** 7 (+3), **Persuasive** 5 (+5), **Quick** 11 (−1), **Resolute** 9 (+1), **Strong** 15 (−5), **Vigilant** 10 (0)

Tactics: Walks straight towards the target or stands at attention by its master.

and features typical to the race, in terms of gender, hair color, voice, cloths and so on but the target keeps its stats, abilities and shadow. Its actual size is not affected, only the size of the illusory appearance.

The illusion cannot be revealed without using other powers or rituals. The only exception is if the target tries to do something he or she normally cannot do, but that the assumed shape could do; then the illusion crumbles. Other than that, the *False Shape* fades away after about a week.

FARAWAY WRITING

Tradition: Symbolism

From a distance the mystic can write signs and symbols in a well-known location. The signs appear on a flat surface, like a wall, a floor or a table. They appear when the mystic performs the ritual, and spell out a short message or even a mystical power from the tradition of *Symbolism*. The mystic can choose to let the writing be visible to all or become visible when a specific individual views the surface. In the latter case, the text appears and/or the power is activated only when that person sees it.

FATA MORGANA

Tradition: Only available to Illusionist

The higher level of the ritual *False Terrain* gives the Illusionist such power over the lie that it touches the truth; that which is created with *Fata Morgana* actually exists, at least during the moon cycle that the illusion persists. The mystic can place a type of terrain over another or decide to raise a smaller building, such as a croft or a stone fort (see Damage on Buildings, page 106), on a select location.

The creation cannot be seen-through but it can be destroyed; if the rules for Damage on Buildings are used, the *Fata Morgana* has half the *Toughness* of a corresponding building. After one month, the illusion fades away over the course of a night. Those who were inside during the night end up on the ground and nothing of the lie remains.

Performing the ritual costs one *Experience* point.

FLESH CRAFT
Tradition: Sorcery

The mystic temporarily transforms his or her hands to flesh crafting and bone sculpting claw-like instruments, put to work on a more or less willing victim. The work transforms the victim into a grotesque mockery of its former self, possessing one or more monstrous traits at level I from the following list: *Acidic Blood, Acidic Attack, Armored, Corrupting Attack, Natural Weapon, Poisonous, Poison Spit, Regeneration, Robust, Wings*. Later, the victim may develop the traits granted by the ritual with *Experience*, as if they were normal abilities.

A voluntary victim gains 1D4 permanent corruption per trait, but is only affected by whatever amount transcends its current value in permanent corruption. An involuntary victim gains 1D4 permanent corruption per trait, which is added to the corruption it already has.

Since the risk of the victim becoming blight born is high, the careful sorcerer always starts off by binding the victim with the ritual *Enslave*. With that precaution taken, the newborn abomination will obey its creator after the fall into darkness.

Example: *The sorceress Agathara uses Flesh Craft on one of her servants, who voluntarily submits to becoming "exalted". She does not know the ritual Enslave, but chains her victim to the wall, just to be on the safe side. The underling has Resolute 12 and permanent corruption 4 when the ritual begins. Agathara opts to give him three monstrous traits, at a total of [3d4−4] in permanent corruption. Agathara rolls 7 on 3d4, giving him 3 more points in permanent corruption, 7 in total. This exceeds his corruption threshold, immediately resulting in an additional 1D4 in permanent corruption. The roll is 3, hence the victim's permanent corruption is 10. Agathara's loyal follower is transformed into an exalted version of himself with three monstrous traits at novice level, without becoming thoroughly corrupt.*

If Agathara had tried to do the same thing to an involuntary victim, the mathematics of corruption would have been grimmer: first, the victim would have suffered 7 in permanent corruption, in addition to the 4 it had, 11

in total – and then suffered 3 more when exceeding the corruption threshold, for a total of 14. Sure, the victim would have received three monstrous traits, but would also have turned into a howling blight beast, out of control. Were it not for the chains, Agathara would most likely have become the newborn's first meal.

LIFE EXTENSION
Tradition: Wizardry

The mystic can postpone his or her aging for a year. The ritual requires one dose of Elixir of Life per use and costs either one *Experience* or a point in permanent corruption.

LIVING FORTRESS
Tradition: Only available to Green Weavers

The higher level of the ritual *Quick Growth* lets the mystic create a fortress of living trees and thorny bushes. The fort counts as a Wooden Fort (see Damage on Buildings, page 106) and defends against anyone trying to pass its living walls – both when entering and exiting. Those trying to pass must succeed with three [Quick←Resolute] tests or suffer 1D12 damage (ignoring armor) per failure from being impaled by thorns or beaten by heavy branches.

The mystic who created the fort can let anyone in or out, and may also teach his or her allies secret words which will let them pass unhindered through the watchful greenery.

The fortress lives a season (three months), then the ritual must be performed again or it will start to wither away. Performing the ritual costs one *Experience* point.

PHYLACTERY
Tradition: Sorcery

The mystic binds his or her corrupt soul to a vessel – usually a figurine – and is physically resurrected in its vicinity within 1D12 days after having died. Creating a *Phylactery* costs either one *Experience* or a point in permanent corruption. Every time the *Phylactery* is used to resurrect the mystic, he or she suffers 1D6 permanent corruption. Thoroughly corrupt creatures cannot have a *Phylactery*, since they technically no longer have a soul.

PIERCING GAZE
Tradition: Only available to Inquisitors

The higher level of the ritual *Holy Smoke* allows the theurg a second chance to pass all tests when using *Holy Smoke*. In addition, with a passed *Cunning* test, the *Piercing Gaze* sees through the ritual *Exchange Shadow*, revealing the actual shadow hidden by the false one.

QUAKE

Tradition: Only available to Staff Mages

It is said that the earth trembles when a staff mage grows furious – likely a rumor brought about by this ritual. The mage draws on the wrath of the bedrock and keeps it stored in his or her rune staff. When needed, the mage can slam the staff into the ground and a force wave shoots out, like waves on water.

The *Quake* can be aimed at a physical structure and then crush doors, windows and bridges; the mystic can strike the targeted structure with the staff, or throw the staff using the power *Staff Projectile*.

No matter if the *Quake* is directed into the ground or towards an object, the mage suffers 1D6 temporary corruption upon activation

Into the ground: The mage strikes the ground and sets off shock waves that topple all creatures nearby with a passed *[Resolute←Quick]* test – one roll per creature, ally or enemy. The mystic and adjacent allies are excluded from the effect, just like any enemies within melee range. Those who fall suffer 1D4 damage, ignoring armor.

Towards an object: The *Quake* is powerful enough to crush bridges, walls and doors. The damage dealt is rolled as a usual hit with the staff, but the quality Razing is added thanks to the ritual; the staff damages structures as if it is a battering ram. See the rule Damage on Buildings, page 106, for more information.

Doors turn to splinters while floors and bridges crumble to dust. If the mystic crushes a floor, he or she remains standing on the edge of the rupture, but before him or her a hole big enough to require two movement actions to get around opens up. Naturally, if it instead is a bridge that is crushed, anyone wanting to pass must climb or swim to the other side.

RAISE UNDEAD

Tradition: Sorcery

The mystic has the ability to grant permanent (un)life to a newly dead creature that perished no more than seven days earlier. For the undead to fall under the mystic's control after the ritual's completion, the mystic must successfully roll a test against *[Resolute←Resolute]*. Should the test fail, the undead awakens with its own will intact and is then free to decide for itself whether or not to follow the mystic. If the test is successful, the creature must obey the mystic as if bound by a slave rune, and can only be freed by the death of its master.

The creature keeps all stats and abilities it had in life and is also gifted with the monstrous trait *Undead* at level I. It does not age but will not go on forever, since its body is in a constant state of slow decomposition. The creature must make a test against *Strong* each year – if the test fails the creature's value in *Strong* is reduced by one point. When the *Strong* value reaches 0, the body finally falls apart and the creature meets its final death.

RESTORE

Tradition: Troll Singing

The mystic can restore a damaged item by singing – a broken sword is mended, a shattered vase is reassembled and a corroded lock regains its functionality. The restored item recovers all its functions and qualities. The mystic cannot create anything new by using the ritual.

RETRIEVE

Tradition: Troll Singing

The mystic can sing a tune that reveals the path to a lost or displaced object. This requires that the mystic, or someone who is in the company of the mystic, knows the object so well that he or she can describe it in detail. If the object in question has been purposefully hidden, the mystic must pass a *[Resolute←Discreet]* test to learn its whereabouts.

RUNE GUARDIAN

Tradition: Symbolism

The mystic creates a personal guard from a statue of stone or wood, carved with life-giving and loyalty building runes. The creator of the guardian can instill some of its own experience into the statue, to make the being stronger upon creation.

The *Rune Guardian* is handled like a second character of the player; it gains *Experience* and develops over time. The guardian does not sleep and has a simple personality, revolving around duty and obedience. If the guardian dies all acquired *Experience* is lost and the mystic must start over with a new guardian.

SEALING/OPENING RITE

Tradition: Troll Singing

The mystic can sing power words over a door, a lock or a gate to either seal it with mystical energies or open it, whether it is locked by a conventional lock or by mystical energies. Sealing a door requires no test, but to open it the mystic must pass a test against *[Resolute←Difficulty]*, where the difficulty is decided by the difficulty of the lock mechanism or the *Resolute* of the mystic who sealed it. Locks that normally cannot be picked, which open to a password or similar, are counted as having Difficulty –8.

RUNE GUARDIAN	
Race	Mystic Being
Resistance	Challenging
Traits	Armored (II), Natural Weapon (II), Robust (III)

Accurate 5 (+5), Cunning 10 (0), Discreet 7 (+3), Persuasive 9 (+1), Quick 10 (0), Resolute 11 (−1), Strong 15 (−5), Vigilant 13 (−3)

Abilities	Iron Fist (adept)
Weapons	Hammer Fists 1D8 (+1D8 for Robust, +1D4 for Iron Fist)
Armor	Stone or wood 1D6 (+1D8 for Robust)
Defense	6
Toughness	15 Pain Threshold 8
Equipment	None
Shadow	Same as the master

Tactics: Obeys its master's commands, seeking the best means to comply.

SERVANT DAEMON		
Race	Abomination	
Resistance	Ordinary	
Traits	Armored (I), Natural Weapon (I)	

Accurate 13 (−3), Cunning 10 (0), Discreet 11 (−1), Persuasive 5 (+5), Quick 15 (−5), Resolute 9 (+1), Strong 7 (+3), Vigilant 10 (0)

Abilities	None	
Weapons	Sharp fangs 1D6 (short)	
Armor	Daemon skin 1D4	
Defense	15	
Toughness	10 Pain Threshold 3	
Equipment	None	
Shadow	Same as the master	

Tactics: Reluctantly obeys its master's commands.

SERVANT DAEMON

Tradition: Only available to Demonologists

The higher level of the ritual *Summon Daemon* binds a servant daemon to the demonologist. The servant is weak at first but can develop over time, and it is handled by the player like a second character. Also, the *Servant Daemon* can be the subject of the ritual *Blood Bond*.

SOUL TRAP

Tradition: Sorcery

With a passed *Resolute* test, the mystic binds the soul of a newly dead creature to a prepared vessel, usually a pendant with a jewel. The target must have died less than a minute prior to the start of the ritual, and the mystic must be at the scene of death or have access to the corpse. The purpose of capturing the soul is often to stop others from contacting it with the ritual *Necromancy*.

The *Soul Trap* is easily destroyed by smashing the vessel, but the rituals *Break Link* and *Exorcism* may also be used if one wants to spare the jewel.

SPELL TRAP

Tradition: Symbolism

The mystic binds a power to a certain location or to an object. Note that the powers of *Symbolism* do not have to be bound this way; this is covered by the Adept level of *Symbolism*. *Spell Trap* is instead used for powers not included in that tradition.

All *Spell Traps* need to be given a trigger criterion when created. Such a criterion can, for instance, be that a living creature enters the room, that someone steps on the *Spell Trap* or that a weapon is drawn in the vicinity. The mystic can exclude him- or herself from being able to trigger the trap, but the allies of the mystic are not excluded – if they meet the criterion, the power is activated.

The mystic who makes the *Spell Trap* does not have to know the power which is to be trapped, but in that case he or she needs the assistance of a mystic who does or a scroll that describes the power. The *Spell Trap* can be dispelled with *Anathema* or the ritual *Break Link*; if not, it remains dormant for years – decades, sometimes centuries – before its energies dissipate.

SPELL TUNNEL

Tradition: Only available to Mentalists

The higher level of the ritual *Clairvoyance* makes it possible for the mentalist to open a mystic tunnel to the location observed. By way of this tunnel, all mystical powers that do not require touching the target can be used. Also the allies of the mentalist can use the tunnel to affect the observed location with mystical powers. However, the tunnel goes both ways, so people on the far side may very well retaliate. Ranged weapons cannot fire projectiles through the tunnel; only powers and traits that work as powers are allowed.

The *Spell Tunnel* is active during a scene but can be closed earlier with *Anathema*.

Daemon Summoning

The three types of daemons are summoned by different rituals; when the mystic acquires the ritual, the type must be specified.

SUMMON DAEMON
(VINDICTIVE, KNOWLEDGEABLE OR GUARDIAN)

Tradition: Only available to Demonologists

Outside the world known to Ambrians and barbarians, winds gust over a dead, mist-covered landscape. Abominations roam the mists, hunting for life to consume. Demonologists know how to summon daemons to the world of the living, and can force them into service. These daemons come in three different forms and the summoning of each requires the use of a separate ritual, but since the procedures share many characteristics they are described together.

Irrespective of the type of daemon to be summoned, the procedure is the same: the creature must appear within a symbol prepared on the ground, and wise demonologists make sure to learn, and use, the ritual *Magic Circle* in order to protect themselves if something goes wrong during the summoning.

Summoning a daemon requires no test to be rolled once the special symbol has been created; however, in order to subdue the daemon and make it obey the demonologist, a test against *[Resolute←Resolute]* must be passed. A blood sacrifice in the form of a living Cultural Being gives the mystic a second chance to pass the test, and if the victim has no permanent corruption the mystic also gains a +1 bonus on the test.

If the test is successful, the daemon does the mystic a service; if the test fails, the daemon is free to do whatever it wishes until the same time next day. The creature cannot stay longer than that unless it is bound to the service of the demonologist. Whether or not the daemon is bound to the mystic, it can never enter magic circles, witch circles or a site protected by *Sanctum*.

The demonologist may only bind one daemon at a time; if more are summoned, the one already bound is freed and will remain in the world for twenty-four hours before returning to its place of origin. However, if the mystic knows more than one of the summoning rituals, he or she can have one daemon of each type in service.

The three rituals let the mystic summon a specific type of daemon – either a Vindictive, a Knowledgeable or a Guardian daemon.

The ritual costs one point in Experience to perform, whether the test to control the daemon is a success or a failure.

Vindictive Daemon: The abomination is one of the winged creatures that soar through the mists of the Yonderworld.

If ordered by the mystic, the Vindictive Daemon can track down and attack a known and named

VINDICTIVE DAEMON	
Manner	Sniffing and prying
Race	Abomination
Resistance	Challenging
Traits	*Armored* (II), *Natural Weapon* (III), *Wings* (III)

Accurate 15 (−5), **Cunning** 10 (0), **Discreet** 13 (−3), **Persuasive** 5 (+5), **Quick** 11 (−1), **Resolute** 7 (+3), **Strong** 9 (+1), **Vigilant** 10 (0)

Abilities	None		
Weapons	Claws 5 (long)		
Armor	Daemon skin 3		
Defense	−1		
Toughness	10	**Pain Threshold**	5
Equipment	None		
Shadow	Like a black, oily cloud dancing in hard winds (thoroughly corrupt)		

Tactics: The daemon will try to wait until the victim is in a location that suits the daemon, preferably a huge open area or a grand hall. It can wait in the shadows or on the beams under the roof to gain *Advantage*. Then it attacks.

creature with the intention of killing it. The mystic needs a link to the target, for example its hair, blood or an item he or she holds dear. The daemon follows the astral link to the victim; if the distance can be counted in day's marches, the daemon flies at death march pace and must test to see if something catastrophic takes place – maybe it is tracked down by witch hunters, or killed by some other monstrosity along the way.

Knowledgeable Daemon: The abomination is one of the manipulative creatures lurking in the mists of the Yonderworld, always looking for lifeforms to tame and consume.

A Knowledgeable Daemon answers one question from the mystic; further *[Resolute←Resolute]* tests provide more answers. The daemon can answer yes or no on a direct question (like the ritual Fortune Telling) or answer an open question (like the ritual *Oracle*). Additional questions do not increase the risk of the daemon breaking free – if a test fails, the daemon will simply refuse to answer more questions – and it takes one hour to get each answer. A blood sacrifice also helps when rolling for additional questions.

Guardian Daemon: The abomination is summoned from among the howling monstrosities that rage through the Yonderworld hunting for targets for their hate and frustration.

KNOWLEDGEABLE DAEMON	
Manner	Fawning and wheezing
Race	Abomination
Resistance	Challenging
Traits	*Alternative Damage* (III)
Accurate 7 (+3), Cunning 10 (0), Discreet 9 (+1), Persuasive 11 (−1), Quick 13 (−3), Resolute 15 (−5), Strong 5 (+5), Vigilant 10 (0)	
Abilities	*Bend Will* (master), *Ritualist* (adept: *Enslave, Oracle, Fortune-telling*)
Weapons	Life-consuming kiss 5, ignores Armor, damages *Resolute*
Armor	None
Defense	−3
Toughness	10 Pain Threshold 3
Equipment	None
Shadow	Calm blackness, like a pool of liquid bitumen (thoroughly corrupt)

Tactics: The daemon will keep its distance and try to bend the will of its victim; when the target no longer manages to resist the daemon consumes its soul. The daemon's greatest wish is to bend the will of the summoning mystic and then Enslave him or her– making it possible for the daemon to remain free in the world, until the mystic dies or is saved from the enslavement.

GUARDIAN DAEMON	
Manner	Snorting and clawing the ground
Race	Abomination
Resistance	Challenging
Traits	*Natural Weapon* (III), *Robust* (II)
Accurate 5 (+5), Cunning 10 (0), Discreet 9 (+1), Persuasive 7 (+3), Quick 13 (−3), Resolute 10 (0), Strong 15 (−5), Vigilant 11 (−1)	
Abilities	*Iron Fist* (adept), *Polearm Mastery* (adept)
Weapons	Claws 11 (long)
Armor	Daemon skin 3
Defense	0
Toughness	15 Pain Threshold 8
Equipment	None
Shadow	Night-black as bubbling and boiling tar (thoroughly corrupt)

Tactics: The daemon will stay within its area of protection and block passage by making full use of its long claws. If the enemy resorts to using ranged attacks, the daemon will enter into melee as soon as possible.

The Guardian Daemon guards a place until it is killed or set free by the demonologist. The daemon will obey instructions regarding who is allowed entry or passage; the demonologist may change the definition regarding who or what may enter or pass, but the pact does not allow him or her to change the location.

TORMENT

Tradition: Witchcraft, Sorcery
The mystic places a tormenting curse on the target. This requires a mystical link to the target. The effect of the ritual can vary, but an often employed version makes the victim slowly wither – its *Toughness* is reduced by one point each week and it cannot heal until the curse is lifted.

Other known effects of the ritual are the summoning of warts or a nasty stench that surrounds the victim, making the target tired during the day and alert at night – then often limited to a duration of a month, just to teach the target a lesson.

The torment effect can be aborted by the ritual *Break Link*.

TRACELESS

Tradition: Witchcraft
All physical traces of the mystic and his or her allies disappear. For instance, footsteps in mud subside, broken branches and grass stalks heal and spider webs are mystically restored. The ritual works just as well in civilization; dust settles on mosaic floors and piles of paper are arranged as they were before the mystic or some ally browsed them.

The duration is 24 hours, either forward or back from the casting of the ritual; traces from the previous day's activities can be obliterated, or the effect can affect all activities performed during the day after the ritual is performed. In any case, the effect of the ritual is that neither the mystic nor his or her allies can be traced by any physical means, including smell. Mystical tracking methods are not affected.

TWIN SERVANTS

Tradition: Only available to Pyromancers
The advanced version of the ritual *Flaming Servant* allows the Pyromancer to have two flaming servants. These are handled like two separate, additional characters by the player, and they gain *Experience* from adventuring just like all flaming servants do.

THUS SPOKE AROALETA

"...and the beings from beyond tore Symbaroum apart, with claws and fangs, horns and spikes; invited but not welcome, called but not wanted; they were the guests who in insatiable hunger ate and drank till there was nothing left to devour ..."

ight fell through cracks in the
ceiling, dancing with the dust
that covered everything in the
room – the bottles of elixirs, poorly
preserved monster trophies and the
matron herself, an aged changeling.

It was Kasimer who had led them
to the cabin. Agniesha remained
by the door, apparently uneasy. Gormyx spoke for the group,
partly because the steady voice of the troll singer made him
a great negotiator, partly because he knew more about the
Underworld then the rest of them combined. Knowledge of the
Abyss was undoubtedly relevant in the situation; their nemesis
had fled there after the confrontation and the group had
decided to hunt him down.

It looked as if the troll and the changeling had already
agreed on a price for a number of items and elixirs, but they
were still squabbling over a brew that the matron claimed
could provide anyone with armor-like skin, claws and even
wings. Gormyx was just about to present a new argument
when Jela heard herself cry out, "I'll take it!" The others gave
her puzzled looks.

In a calmer voice she explained, *"I'll take it. I'd rather die
than allow the black priest to escape again!"*

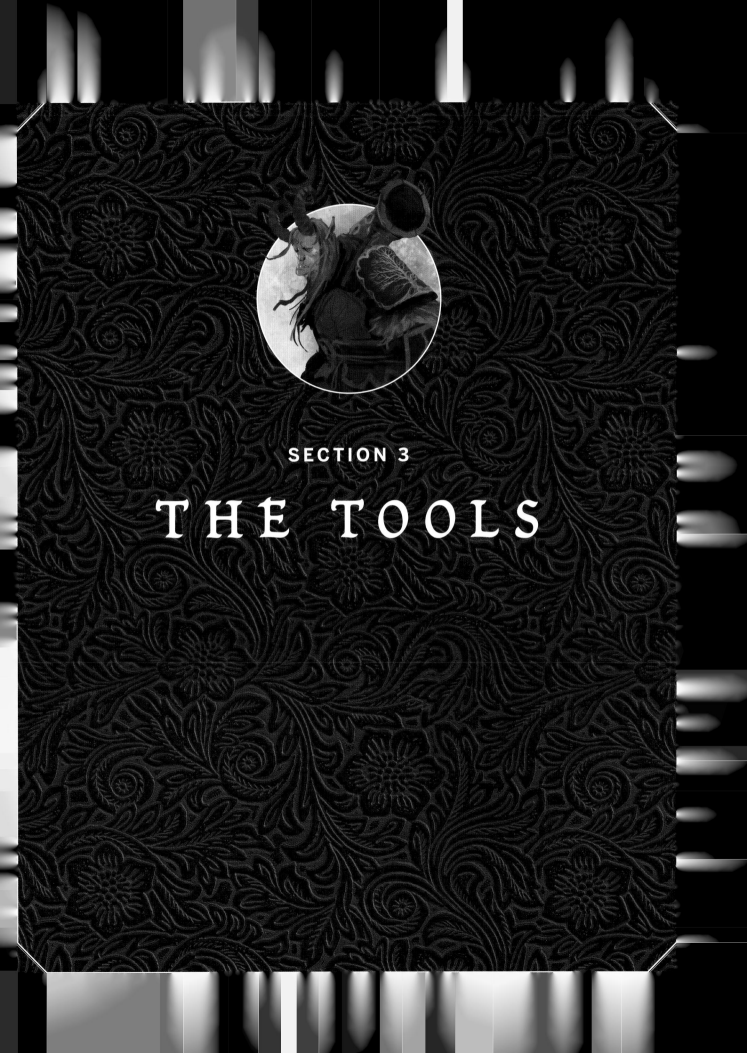

SECTION 3

THE TOOLS

Alternative Rules

THIS SECTION PRESENTS a number of new rules and mechanics. Most of them are optional or introduced as alternatives, while a few present additions and clarifications needed to play with the abilities included in this book. As always, all alternative rules should be discussed within the gaming group and approved by the Game Master before being used; after all, they affect everyone, including the task of the GM.

Untrained Use of Alchemical Weapons

The alchemical weapons which may be used by anyone entail a measure of risk for the untrained – a success test with the outcome 20 (or if used against the characters, a *Defense* test with the outcome 1) means that the weapon detonates in the hands of the user. The user then takes full damage, without rolling for *Defense*. Also, everyone in direct contact with the user must roll *Defense* or suffer half the damage. Trained users do not risk such catastrophic failures.

ALCHEMICAL WEAPONS

Many alchemical weapons can be used by anyone, but only those with the proper training can do so without risk. The more advanced types cannot be used at all without the proper training. Here is a summary of what applies:

Alchemical Fire Tube (portable): requires *Siege Expert* (adept) to be used without risk.

Alchemical Fire Tube (stationary): requires *Siege Expert* (adept) to be used at all.

Alchemical Grenade: requires *Alchemy*, *Siege Expert* or *Pyrotechnics* to be used without risk.

Alchemical Mine: requires either *Trapper* or *Pyrotechnics* to be used at all.

Breaching Pot: Anyone can make use of a Breaching Pot, but only a person with the ability *Siege Expert* or *Pyrotechnics* can do so without risk.

DISTANCE CATEGORIES

Some gaming groups find the basic rules for ranged weapons too simplistic since they do not take distance into account; the shooter must simply be able to see the enemy and have a clear line of sight to it. If your gaming group wants more nuanced and tactically relevant rules, the following guidelines may be used:

Each combat encounter starts at a distance determined by the situation and terrain (the GM decides). The distance categories modify damage and the chance to hit, and correspond to the number of movement actions needed for the combatants to engage each other in melee combat.

Note that mystical powers are not in any way affected by this rule.

An obvious effect of the rule is that characters with ranged weapons cannot fight effectively at short range; they have to move (and suffer Free Attacks) or switch weapons. This means that the abilities *Acrobatics*, *Arrow Jab* and *Quick Draw* become even more valuable.

TURN UNDEAD INSTEAD OF DEAD

The undead are a plague that spreads throughout Ambria and Davokar. The reason for this is unknown, but theories speak of the *"twilight of the world"* and the *"imminent collapse of the natural order."*

For those gaming groups who are so inclined, there is the possibility for characters who are killed to become undead instead, and then remain in play. This optional rule can be combined with the alternative rule Direct Kill, which would further increase the chance/risk of a character becoming undead.

Another option is to let the player whose character dies roll a test to become undead instead, preferably a simple *Resolute* test.

TURN UNDEAD INSTEAD OF THOROUGHLY CORRUPT

An implicit fact in *Symbaroum* is that some creatures can be thoroughly corrupt without losing their will entirely. If the gaming group wishes, the same may apply to sorcerers – instead of becoming blight-born when thoroughly corrupt, they may roll a *Resolute* test to become undead, in accordance with the race introduced in the *Advanced Player's Guide*.

FEATS

Introducing rules for feats may be an intriguing option for gaming groups wanting the player characters to be more like traditional heroes. In short, feats are actions that only especially heroic individuals can accomplish. However, it should be noted that this gives the characters access to actions which seriously tip the game balance in their favor. Of course, in heroic gaming this is kind of the point.

Feats cost one (1) *Experience* – or one (1) permanent corruption – to activate.

Clean Hit: The hero makes a normal attack and the successful hit or hits deal maximum damage.

Fearless: The hero ignores horror effects, like from the monstrous trait *Terrify*.

Ignore Corruption: During the rest of the turn, the accumulated corruption of the hero does not matter; all tests are made as if he or she had zero corruption. However, the hero suffers corruption as usual, which comes into play the following turn.

Perfect Defense: The hero parries or dodges a successful attack that otherwise would have hit him or her. Perfect Defense may only be used once per turn.

Quick Strike: The hero attacks first in the turn. If someone else is using Quick Strike, the order of initiative is settled in the normal way.

Resilience: +1D4 *Armor* for the rest of the turn.

Steely Gaze: The hero's gaze makes an enemy step back and refrain from attacking the hero. If the fight is already on, the enemy may choose to attack another creature; if the fight has not started, the enemy will not attack before someone else deals the first blow.

Whirlwind Attack: In one combat action, the hero performs one attack against each enemy engaged in melee.

Alchemical Weapons

By the end of The Great War, when the balance of power was still even and the outcome undecided, the army strategists of Korinthia sent two fast sailing ships hunting for a rumor. Spies and far-travelled merchants spoke of alchemical weapon types with terrible destructive power, developed by the City States and used in combat against each other as well as against a common enemy (giants according to some, elves and abominations according to others). The ships returned full of such weapons.

The simplest type of alchemical weapon is the grenade. There are also more massive contraptions, in the form of missile batteries firing swarms of fire arrows and huge fire tubes that spew burning death at the enemy. During the final days of battle, the alchemy masters of Ordo Magica attempted to improve the imported innovations – for instance they experimented with solid cast fire tubes that could be reloaded after each use instead of burning up, like the imported ones made from wood. The masters were very successful and the tubes made from metal quickly became the standard, soon followed by portable types that could be handled by individual sappers on foot.

Right before the end of the war, when Korinthia was held captive, the desperate War Council also acquired two massive weapons from the city state Koral. They did not arrive in time to contribute during the storming of the Dark Lords' fortress, but they were brought along over the Titans – "The Volcano" kept in Agrella and the missile battery called "The Four Horsemen" stored with the Sapper Corps of Yndaros.

Alchemical weapons are still uncommon in Ambria. They are expensive and few in number, since both Ordo Magica and the rest of the realm have focused on other tasks after the end of the war; most of the fire tubes now used by sappers and panzer alchemists came with the caravans from old Alberetor. But this may very well be about to change. Much seems to indicate that grenades as well as fire tubes and missile batteries will become crucial when and if the Queen decides that the time has come to penetrate deeper into Davokar.

Table 6: Distance Categories

DISTANCE CATEGORY	EFFECT ON RANGED WEAPONS	APPROX. DISTANCE	NUMBER OF MOVEMENTS
Close	Attack is only possible in the first turn and only if the shooter has the initiative	1–2 meters	None
Short	+2 on attack test, +1D4 in damage	10 meters	1
Medium	None	20 meters	2
Long	−2 on attack test	50 meters	5
Extreme	−5 on attack test	100 meters	10

ENCUMBRANCE

For the gaming groups who like the idea, an encumbrance rule may be introduced, specifying how much characters can carry without being hampered.

There are limits to how much a character can carry. To decide if he or she becomes exhausted by moving around laden with treasures, masterly crafted barbarian axes or gold-plated armor, the items are abstractly measured in numbers rather than in weight. A character can carry a number of items mirroring his or her *Strong* value without being negatively affected. If the character carries more, each extra item gives a –1 modification to *Defense*, just like the impeding effect of armor.

A character can carry a maximum of *Strong* ×2 items; after that he or she cannot move more than short distances at a time.

With the boon *Pack-mule*, the encumbrance limit is calculated as *Strong* x1.5 instead, rounded down. Besides these basics the following applies:

- Clothing, belts and boots do not count as carried items
- Backpacks, sacks, shoulder-bags and other light containers do not count as items; only the contents are counted
- Barrels, chests, boxes and other bulky containers count as items in their own right, adding to what they contain
- Smaller objects (coins, pendants, jewels) weigh nothing unless one carries a lot of them; they count as one carried item for every 50 pieces
- Armor worn for protection does not count in this case; it has an impeding value instead. Armor which is carried but not worn for protection correspond to a number of items equal to its impeding value
- Weapons held in a character's hands do not count as carried items (but signal hostility). Weapons carried in the pack, in their sheaths or similar are encumbering.
- Weapons with the quality Massive count as two items.

A character who carries more than allowed will also have a hard time keeping pace during longer marches – the categories in table 27 on page 184 in *Symbaroum's Core Rulebook* grow one tier worse when a character carries too much. A Day's March counts as a Forced March, and a Forced March counts as a Death March. An encumbered character cannot travel at true Death March pace. Furthermore, the heavy load gives a –1 modification per extra item to *Strong* when rolling to see if the Death March results in 1 or 1+1D6 damage per day's travel.

The monastery of the Twilight Friars, seen from one of the Titan's many valleys.

RESEARCH IN ARCHIVES

Anyone can search for information in archives and libraries, but in order to find anything useful they obviously need to search in a place where the desired information can be found (in other words, searching for directions to Symbar at the town archives of Thistle Hold is hopeless). Learning where to search may require a passed *Cunning* test in combination with suitable *Contacts*.

In practice, the search is based on the characters directing a question to the document collection. If the Game Master deems that the documents may contain some relevant information, a character with the ability *Loremaster* rolls against *Cunning* while the others roll a *[Cunning –5]* test. A character with the boon *Archivist* gains a second chance to pass all tests when searching document collections.

Each character partaking in the research may roll; the one with the best chance to succeed starts, then the rest follow in descending order. If the test fails it is over and that character has to continue searching somewhere else, but if someone passes the test, the Game Master should deliver an answer to the question.

If the answer lies inside a specific field of knowledge covered by some other ability, this ability may be used instead of *Loremaster* when researching: abilities such as *Alchemy*, *Artifact Crafting*, *Poisoner*, *Medicus*, *Beast Lore* and diverse versions of *Mystical Traditions* can be relevant in this context. If the answer to the question is complex, these abilities may also provide deeper insights according to the rule on Degrees of Success, described on page 172 in the *Core Rulebook*.

START WITH FREE EXPERIENCE

In the *Core Rulebook*, on page 179, is the optional rule Re-roll for Experience. With that in mind, and because of the new possibilities introduced by the rules on boons and burdens, some gaming groups may prefer to build their characters in another way than what is described in the *Core Rulebook* – that is, to begin with free *Experience* instead of choosing one ability at adept level and two at novice level (alternately five at novice level).

Starting with free *Experience* means that each player gets 50 *Experience* points to use for his or her character. This can be increased by choosing burdens and then spent to acquire boons, abilities and traits. However, the *Experience* may also be saved for re-rolls, if the optional rule Re-roll for Experience is used by the group.

MORE RITUALS FOR MASTERS

The ability *Ritualist* has a limit of six rituals when reaching the master level. For gaming groups that really enjoy rituals and think that half a dozen is too few for a true master ritualist, the following alternative rule is recommended:

Master ritualists can learn additional rituals for the cost of 10 *Experience* points per ritual. Only a master can acquire more rituals this way; for less prominent ritualists, what is detailed in the description of the ability levels applies.

FLIGHT & HUNT

When the characters are trying to escape anyone or anything hunting them, it is suggested that the Game Master handles it based on the attribute *Quick*. If the characters decide to stick together, the one with the lowest value in *Quick* must make a test, modified by the *Quick* of the fastest hunter. Should they split up, all of them need to make a test, again modified by the *Quick* of the fastest hunter. If it is the other way around and the characters are on the hunt the same formula is used, but instead with a modification based on the slowest prey.

During the hunt, one test is made each turn – if the prey succeeds it pulls away one step, if the prey fails the hunter comes one step closer. To finally get away, the hunted must reach an advantage of 3, in other words, he or she must succeed at three rolls more than he or she fails. And the prey who fails at three rolls more than he or she succeeds will of course get caught.

Example: *The barbarian thief Hoska almost got away after a burglary in Thistle Hold when a lone watchman saw him exit the building – the hunt begins! Hoska has Quick 13 and the guard Quick 9 (+1), meaning that Hoska's player must roll against 13+1=14 in an attempt to escape the hunter.*

In the first turn, the player rolls a 7 – Hoska pulls away and has advantage 1. The luck holds and the second dice roll lands on 13: advantage 2. One more successful roll and Hoska is free. But unfortunately, the third roll is 17; the guard comes closer and the advantage is 1. Hoska's player sighs nervously. The hunt goes on!

TRAPS

Trained as well as untrained characters can set traps, in order to protect a location or slow an enemy down. Here follows rules on portable traps and those which may be constructed on location.

Specific traps are described in the chapter Equipment on page 127.

Setting a Trap

With a passed *Cunning* test, the character can set a ready-made trap.

Untrained individuals (i.e. those who do not have the ability *Trapper*) can only set mechanical traps, which require a passed *Cunning* test. If the outcome of the test is 20, the trap is sprung in their faces.

Trained trappers can ready both mechanical traps and alchemical mines with a combat action, and they can also craft improvised traps. This requires the ability *Trapper*, or *Pyrotechnics* if only using alchemical mines.

Discovering a Trap

Anyone at risk of activating a trap discovers it with a passed *[Vigilant←Discreet]* test.

Bypassing a Trap

A discovered trap can be bypassed in two ways:

It can be jumped over as part of a movement action, which requires a *[Quick←Cunning]* test. If the test fails, the trap is sprung and the character is caught by it, i.e. movement is interrupted.

If the terrain allows, a trap can always be ignored by going around it. This costs an extra movement action, or more depending on the terrain.

Disarming a Trap

A discovered trap can also be disarmed.

An untrained individual cannot disarm traps – they have to incapacitate them by shooting or poking at them with a long instrument (the quality Long). The procedure counts as a combat action and requires a passed *[Accurate←Cunning]* test.

An individual with the ability *Trapper* can roll a *[Cunning←Cunning]* test to disarm a trap, and does not require an instrument with the quality Long to do so.

Getting Free from a Trap

Traps often deal damage, specified in the description of the trap or, in the case of improvised traps, in the description of the ability *Trapper*. Furthermore, if the trap has such qualities it may hold the victim in place. If so, this is mentioned in the description, combined with information on what it takes to get free.

TRADE IN USED GOODS AND TREASURES

Sometimes the player characters will want to sell goods in the form of used weapons and armor. Merchants will gladly buy such secondhand items at half of the listed price (then give them a polish and sell them to someone else at full price).

Items with mystical qualities tend to keep their value over time and are always sold at a price corresponding to the listed price. Also, normal trade items are sold at the listed purchase price, making such finds into cumbersome but valuable treasures.

INCOME FROM BOONS

For gaming groups who like to see the characters use the time in-between adventures actively, boons may be used as a source of income.

The most obvious boons to be used this way are *Cartographer, Cheat, Escape Artist, Gambler, Impressionist, Medium, Mirage, Musician* and *Storyteller*. Other boons and abilities may of course be used to earn thaler, if the player can give a reasonable explanation as to how.

Once per adventure (or in-between adventures), the player may roll against the attribute related to the boon/ability; if there is no such attribute, use the highest of *Cunning* or *Persuasive*. A passed test renders an income of 1D10 thaler.

MANEUVERS

For gaming groups looking to add more tactical choices to the game, maneuvers may be an attractive addition, giving more options to everyone involved in combat. Of course, a drawback is that this makes combat scenes much more complicated, both with regard to the number of choices that players have to make and the book-keeping required by the Game Master. In essence, it will take longer to play out a combat scene; some gaming groups see this as a benefit, others do not.

In some cases, maneuvers work much like abilities and can blur the line between abilities and tactical choices available to everyone. Sure, the abilities are always much more powerful, but you should still take some time to discuss if you want to add this mechanic or not.

Some of the maneuvers will only be useful if the gaming group also uses the optional rule Movement by Scale (page 181 in the *Core Rulebook*), or is at least willing to play with a simplified Combat map (page 162 in the *Core Rulebook*).

Here follows a list of maneuvers that all characters and opponents may employ, hoping to improve their own position or make things harder for the enemy.

Careful Aiming

You take the time to aim carefully with a ranged weapon and get a second chance to pass the attack test. The cost is a movement action, meaning that you cannot move during the turn.

Charge

You charge at the enemy and make a double movement plus a combat action in melee. The charge must be in a straight line towards the target. If the attack test fails, the target gets to make a Free Attack.

Delay the Initiative

You choose to delay your initiative during the turn, to let someone else go first. When it is your time to act, you specify who will get to act before you. The next turn, you are back at your normal place in the order of initiative.

Disarm

You attack the enemy's weapon or shield, hoping to make him or her drop it *[Accurate←Strong]*. The attack deals no damage, and if the test fails you expose yourself to a Free Attack from the enemy.

Full Defense

You stake everything on defense and have a second chance to pass all *Defense* tests during the turn. You are not allowed to perform any attacks.

Full Offense

You stake everything on melee attacks for a turn, giving you a second chance to pass all melee attacks. Because of this you simultaneously have a second chance to fail all *Defense* test during the turn.

Hold

You attack with a wrestling maneuver aimed at stopping the target from moving *[Strong←Strong]*. The trait *Robust* gives a bonus to the test, +2 at level I, +4 at level II and +8 at level III. This modification applies to both the wrestler and its target, if the latter is *Robust*. A test is made each turn to maintain the hold.

If the test fails, the target gets to make a Free Attack. Also, note that you cannot perform any other actions while maintaining the hold.

Knock Out

You attack from an *Advantage*, aiming to render the target unconscious. The attack is made as usual, but instead of dealing damage, 1D12 is rolled against the damage value; if the outcome is lower than the value, the target is knocked out. If the attack fails, you lose the *Advantage* over the target (see page 162 in the *Core Rulebook* for more on *Advantage*).

Example: *Grumpa has snuck-up on a guard and tries to knock him out. The attack is successful; the damage die is rolled with the outcome 6. Grumpa's player rolls 1D12, trying to roll under 6; she rolls a 4 and the guard falls unconscious to the ground.*

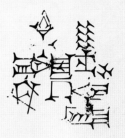

Writings carved on a stone close to the Marshes, possibly a message to travelers in the area, warning them of hostile elves.

Poison on Weapons

With a passed *Cunning* test, you may use a combat action to apply poison to your weapon. If the outcome is 20 something goes wrong and you yourself are poisoned.

The poison is enough for one hit, then a new dose must be applied.

Push Back

You lunge at the target with the intention of pushing it backwards – out of a room, over the edge of a cliff or similar. You have to start your turn with the push and must spend both your combat and your movement action doing so. A passed attack test deals half damage but will also push the target half a movement back (five meters). If the test fails, the target gets to make a Free Attack.

Tackle

You attack hoping to knock down the target [Strong←Strong]. The risk is that you also topple over, whether you make a successful tackle or not; a passed *Quick* test lets you remain standing. The tackle counts as your combat action and if you are *Robust* you add +2 to the *Strong* test per level acquired in the trait.

Take the Initiative

You roll a *Resolute* test hoping to gain the initiative. If successful you gain a +5 bonus when deciding your place in the order of initiative. The downside is that your speed has a negative impact on your precision; you have a second chance to fail all success test during the turn, no matter if the *Resolute* test was successful or not. The next turn, you are back to your normal place in the order of initiative.

MONSTER TROPHIES

For anyone who slays monsters and collects trophies there is money to earn, even if the procurement of the valuable parts can cause problems for the untrained – putrefaction spoils many trophies completely and lowers the price on others. A *Cunning* test is required to be able to harvest a trophy, rendering a trophy in poor condition if successful and no trophy at all if failed. To end up with a trophy in good condition, a passed *Cunning* test with the ability *Beast Lore* or the boon *Bushcraft* is needed; if such a test fails, a trophy in poor condition is harvested instead.

At the bottom of the page is a list of obvious and more exotic trophies that monster hunters can collect during their hunting trips into the woods.

MASTERCRAFTED ITEMS

During their adventures, the player characters may happen upon master crafted weapons and armor, and should they instead find valuables or coin they have the opportunity to buy mastercrafts from especially skilled blacksmiths.

The master smith has the ability to add one or more qualities to the object in question, or alternatively to remove negative qualities. For every added or removed quality, the cost/value of the item is cumulatively increased by ×5. Mystical qualities cumulatively increase the price by ×10.

Example: *If a sword costs five thaler, a master craft version with the quality Deep Impact would be worth 25 thaler (5×5 thaler). If you also want that sword to be Precise, the value is ramped up to 125 thaler (5×5×5 thaler). And if you also want it to be Flaming, the price is 1 250 thaler (5×5×5×10 thaler), truly a weapon for kings and queens!*

PACT-MAKING

To enter into a pact with one of the ancient powers of the world can be a shortcut to knowledge and power – but it is far from risk-free. To commoners, pact-making and sorcery are more or less the same, but even if many sorcerers use pacts as a means to grow stronger anyone who is brave or desperate enough can enter into a pact.

Pact-making requires an agreement with a mighty being who is interested in becoming the character's protector and tutor; usually a nature spirit or an undead.

Table 7: Monster Trophies

RESISTANCE	EXAMPLE	VALUE (GOOD/POOR CONDITION)
Weak	A set of jakaar teeth	1 thaler/–
Ordinary	The black skin of a mare cat or a tricklesting pinned to a canvas	10 thaler/1 thaler
Challenging	A pair of dragon fly wings or an aboar skull	100 thaler/10 thaler
Strong	The hypnotic eyes of a lindworm	500 thaler/50 thaler
Mighty	The cranium of an arch troll	1 000 thaler/100 thaler

In short, this being imbues the character with some of its power, to gain a loyal agent who can reach places that the being cannot, or with the long-term goal of consuming the spiritual force of the character when he or she finally turns blight born – or sometimes both. In the first case, the character will be forced to act in a way which furthers a goal that the being strives for; in the second case, the being will try to tempt the character into attracting and amassing corruption in any way it can.

The Benefits of the Pact

The character can gain *Experience* in exchange for accepting permanent corruption; each point in permanent corruption gives 1D12 *Experience* points. This happens when the pact is forged. Later a maximum of 1 permanent corruption per adventure can be accepted. The player decides if and when this exchange will be made.

The character gains access to all monstrous traits, abilities, mystical powers and rituals that the being has. He or she must pay for these gifts with *Experience* as usual.

The character can also gain access to other traits and abilities, besides the ones possessed by the being. In that case, the gift must be paid for with 1 point in permanent corruption, a point that does not provide additional *Experience*. Once the gift has been paid for, it must be acquired by spending *Experience* as usual.

The Price of the Pact

The character must accept one of the being's goals as his or her own and strive towards it. This goal may either replace one of the character's own goals, or be assumed as an additional goal for the character. Either way, the goal is determined when the pact is forged.

The character can no longer have personal goals which contradict the being's objectives. This is also made clear when the pact is forged, and a requirement for reaching an agreement at all.

If the character starts to divert from or act in disagreement with the being's goals and objectives, the being will know this. Initially, the character will be warned in the form of nightmares, physical discomfort or similar. Then, if the character does not change his or her ways, things will go from bad to worse; the being will deny the character the choice to exchange corruption for *Experience* and put a curse on him or her – either meaning that all corruption gained by the character is doubled or that he or she cannot heal naturally and that all other healing is halved. Another option is that all the oath-breaker's rolls against his or her most

frequently used attribute gain a second chance to fail. The being will choose the alternative which is most damaging to the character.

Breaking a Pact

There is no known way to break this sort of pact. You can temporarily hide from the pact and the curse in a witch circle, a magic circle or inside a sanctum (see the rituals in question for details). However, as soon as the character steps outside such a location, the curse returns in full force.

DAMAGE ON BUILDINGS

There will likely be times when the characters are in a hurry to force a physical obstacle, or it may be the enemies who need to do the same in order to reach the characters.

New concepts related to buildings are needed:

Toughness: When the *Toughness* of a building reaches zero it is accessible to the attacker: a fortification crumbles, a wall collapses and so on. The breach is big enough for 1D4 attackers to enter per turn, against defenders who can stand four abreast across the newly formed opening.

Breakpoint: If a building is dealt half of its *Toughness* in damage in one turn – i.e. the Breakpoint is exceeded – it is immediately breached. Note that this includes all damage dealt during the turn, not from a single attack as is the case with the *Pain Threshold*. Hence, with enough catapults gathered, the walls of a castle can be breached in a single turn, at least in theory.

Fortification: In essence, Fortification is the *Armor* of the building. Weapons with the quality Wrecking ignore the Fortification value; other weapons must first penetrate the Fortification value before damaging the structure. Abilities with an armor penetrating effect have no such effect on buildings.

Set Buildings on Fire

Setting wooden buildings on fire is an often used tactic during sieges. This requires some kind of flammable concoction – it can be an alchemical grenade, a flaming oil canister or a simple fire made from dry twigs and tinder. When the building has been exposed to the flames, a test against [*Cunning –Fortification*] is rolled to see if it catches fire; if so, the flames deal 1D4 damage and count as having the quality Wrecking. Note that whoever lights the fire will become the target of ranged attacks, provided that the building in question has windows or archers on the roof.

Those inside a burning building are at risk of suffering damage each turn the building continues to burn – a passed *Strong* test per turn is required, or else the individual starts taking 1D4 damage (ignoring *Armor*) each turn from fumes and heat. When a *Strong* test has failed the damage continues automatically; the only way to stop it is to leave the building or find some other way to cool down.

Putting out the fire once it has begun to spread requires access to massive amounts of water, sand or similar. The fire dies when someone succeeds with a test against *[Cunning –the number of turns the fire has raged after the first]*. Anyone who extinguishes the fire in this way will likely become the target of ranged attacks.

RECLAIMING BOLTS AND ARROWS
Some gaming groups may find it realistic and desirable if arrows and bolts which have been fired during combat are at risk of breaking – this makes it important for archers to plan ahead (the projectiles become a resource) and it also makes it worthwhile to spend some time searching for undamaged projectiles after the battle, muttering in anger each time one of them proves to be fractured or destroyed in some other way.

Groups who want rules for reclaiming used projectiles can use these guidelines.

- An ordinary projectile proves to be damaged if the player rolls over 10 with 1D20. This applies to all projectiles without qualities.
- A projectile with some kind of quality (e.g. Balanced or Deep Impact) is damaged if the player rolls over 15 with 1D20.
- Projectiles with mystical qualities are damaged if the player rolls over 17 with 1D20.

THE SECRETS OF THE TRADITIONS
The mystical traditions harbor secrets that they are reluctant to share with outsiders. The rules on alchemy and artifacts do not take this secrecy into account, but gaming groups who wish to use the creative abilities in line with the traditions of the game world are welcome to use the rules described here.

The secret recipes and procedures are known only to characters initiated in the different traditions, but can be used by anyone who has gained access to them while playing – whether they have acquired the knowledge from a tutor, found mysterious texts on the subject or purchased the secrets from the black market in Thistle Hold or some other town.

If this rule is used, every alchemist or artifact-crafter must choose which tradition to belong to.

Note that the boon Forbidden Knowledge can give a character access to the secrets of all traditions from the start.

Table 8: Damage on Buildings

BUILDING	TOUGHNESS	BREAKPOINT	FORTIFICA-TION VALUE*
Croft	10	5	5
Farm house	10	5	10
Guard Tower, wood	10	5	15
Guard Tower, stone	40	20	20
Fort, wood	50	25	15
Manor	100	50	10
Fort, stone	200	100	20
Stronghold	500	250	20
Castle	1000	500	20

*Weapons with the quality Wrecking ignore the building's Fortification value and damage its *Toughness* directly. Abilities with an armor penetrating effect have no such effect on buildings.

Secrets of Witchcraft
- **Alchemy:** Transformation Brew, Thorn Beasties
- **Artifact Crafting:** Bark Mask, Witch Braid, Beast Mask, Burial Shroud
- **Blacksmith:** Blood-letting, Retributive, Witch Gown

Secrets of Wizardry
- **Alchemy:** Alchemical Grenade
- **Artifact Crafting:** Alchemical Mine, Spell Scroll, Spell Seal, Spark Stone, Ruler's Ring, Order Medallion, Mind Prism
- **Blacksmith:** Flaming, Order Cloak, Poison Coated

Secrets of Symbolism
- **Alchemy:** War Paint
- **Artifact Crafting:** Ritual Codex, Ritual Seal, Transcendental Weapon
- **Blacksmith:** Bane Weapon

Secrets of Staff Magic
- **Alchemy:** None
- **Artifact Crafting:** Rune Staff, Staff Foot, Staff Head
- **Blacksmith:** Acid Coated

Secrets of Sorcery
- **Alchemy:** Spirit Friend, Shadow Tint, Homunculus
- **Artifact Crafting:** Death Mask, Iron Crown
- **Blacksmith:** Concealed Armor, Death Rune and Desecrated

Main Hand

If Hit Locations are used, it might be wise to decide if the characters are right- or left-handed. As a suggestion, the character has the same main hand as its player and all NPCs are assumed to be right-handed.

Table 9: Hit Locations

1D10	BODY PART	EFFECT OF DAMAGES EQUAL TO OR HIGHER THAN PAIN THRESHOLD
1	Right Leg	Knocked prone. Half movement for the rest of the scene.
2	Left Leg	Knocked prone. Half movement for the rest of the scene.
3–5	Torso	Loses breath; incapacitated for a turn.
6–7	Right Arm	Drops item held if failing a *Quick* test. Also, a second chance to fail all rolls requiring the use of the arm for the rest of the scene.
8–9	Left Arm	Drops item held if failing a *Quick* test. Also, a second chance to fail all rolls requiring the use of the arm for the rest of the scene.
10	Head	+1D6 damage and the target is rendered unconscious for 1D4 turns

Secrets of Theurgy
- **Alchemy:** Holy Water
- **Artifact Crafting:** Pest Mask, Sun Mask
- **Blacksmith:** Blessed Robe, Hallowed

Secrets of Troll Singing
- **Alchemy:** None
- **Artifact Crafting:** Healing Spider, Lucky Coin, Marlit Cape, Meeting Stone, Toad Guard
- **Blacksmith:** Skald's Cuirass, Thundering

HIT LOCATIONS
This optional rule makes it possible to hit specific parts of the enemy and means that damage equal to or higher than the *Pain Threshold* has different effects depending on where the enemy is hit. Also, armor may be divided into segments so that the character can have different types of armor on different parts of the body.

Aim High or Low
The character can choose to aim high or low in order to hit unprotected parts of the target, or to cause a certain effect - for instance that the target loses a movement action or drops something. Aiming high or low gives –2 on the attack test.

Aim at Body Part
The character can take aim at a specific part of the enemy's body, hoping to hit a less protected area or achieve a specific effect. Aiming at a specific body part gives –5 on the success test.

Armor Segments
The character can use different armor on different body parts, to save money and reduce the level of impediment while still protecting the most vital parts as much as possible.

Armor segments cost a part of the price of the full armor and have a part of the armor's value in Impeding. The impediment is rounded up so that 0.5 becomes 1.

Aim High or Low

1D10 HIGH:

1	Right Leg
2	Left Leg
3–4	Torso
5–6	Right Arm
7–8	Left Arm
9–10	Head

1D10 LOW:

1–2	Right Leg
3–4	Left Leg
5–7	Torso
8	Right Arm
9	Left Arm
10	Head

Table 10: Armor Segments

ARMOR SEGMENT	PRICE/IMPEDING VALUE
Legs	20 % (10 % per leg)
Curiass (torso)	40 %
Arms	20 % (10 % per arm)
Helmet	20 %

REPUTATION
In the world of *Symbaroum* there are lots of adventurous people, and some of these live long enough to become famous - or infamous. Such fame is, however, a double-edged sword: sure, being renowned will give you certain social benefits, but it also makes it much harder to travel or act without being noticed. Furthermore, there will be many rumors circling about, detailing the deeds and happenings the character is known for. Regardless of the rumors' veracity, people will treat the character differently - being famous is seldom all good, but with a certain kind of people it is also true that being infamous may work in your favor.

The value in Reputation states how well-known the character is and has the following effects:
- Reputation modifies *Discreet* negatively when the character tries to avoid attention.
- Reputation modifies *Persuasive* negatively when the character tries to influence a supporter from a hostile faction, if the character is recognized and identified because of his or her reputation.
- Reputation modifies *Persuasive* positively if the character mentions his or her name and deeds when trying to earn social favors.

Changes in Reputation
The character can influence his or her reputation primarily by adventuring, but also by encouraging

Table 11: Reputation

VALUE	TYPE	EXAMPLE
0	Commoners	—
1	Upstanding commoner	Kadra, treasure hunter in Thistle Hold
2	Experienced adventurer	Lysindra Goldengrasp, successful treasure hunter
3	Locally acknowledged hero	Garm Wormwriggler, the goblin hero in Thistle Hold
4	Widely known hero	Serex Attio, aged war hero from The Great War
5	Prominent leader	Iakobo Vearra, Commander of the templars in The Knights of the Dying Sun
6	Ambria's dukes	Esmerelda, the Queen's sister and duchess of Kasandrien
7	Legendary individual	Lasifor Nightpitch, Mayor of Thistle Hold; Yeleta, the Huldra of Karvosti
9	—	Tharaban, High Chieftain of the barbarian clans
10	—	Korinthia Nightbane, Queen of Ambria

Table 12: Changes in Reputation

ACTIVITY	EFFECT ON REPUTATION
Ordinary adventuring	±0. One adventure per season (four per year) is enough to uphold the reputation (for instance the adventures in The Copper Crown: *The Promised Land*, *The Mark of the Beast* and *Tomb of Dying Dreams*)
Public adventuring	+1 per adventure with a significant public impact, in a town or with great effect on a large area (for instance *Wrath of the Warden*)
Heroic Tales/Songs	+1 to the cost of 10 thaler, to a maximum of +1 in Reputation. A character with the boon *Storyteller* or *Musician* can get this bonus for free
A thorough introduction	+1 in the present situation but no effect beyond that
Absence, rest or silence	−1 per season of rest or silence (four per year); including adventures which completely escapes the public

the spread of rumors, songs and tales. On the other hand, the character may also make an effort to act discreetly, hoping to avoid becoming famous. Surely, being recognized is not in every character's best interest.

Type of Reputation

Aside from the numerical value, a character's reputation should be suitably described in the form of an epithet and a short sentence or two. As previously mentioned, the details of the reputation can complicate things, depending on who you interact with – the epithet "The Savior of Thistle Hold" will likely provoke other reactions than "The Oathbreaker", and would surely inspire to very diverse sentiments with people from different factions. A reputation as a "Witch Killer" will earn the character a warm welcome in Templewall and certain parts of Yndaros, while the welcome would be quite different on Karvosti or when meeting witches deep inside Davokar.

In short: the reputation of the character will affect how he or she is regarded by others and provoke different reactions from different people.

OVERLAPPING EFFECTS

When a character acts in a way which leads to overlapping effects, the following applies:

- **A second chance to pass/fail a success test:** Only one extra roll is made, no matter how many such effects are in play and what rule they derive from.
- **Simultaneous second chance to pass and fail:** The effects cancel each other out, and an extra roll is only made if the character has more of one than the other.
- **Multiple positive and negative modifications on the same success test:** These are added together, but only one modifier from each type of source – boons, items, elixirs – may be used. If several modifications stem from the same source (i.e. many items that gives a bonus on the same test), only the highest modification comes into play.
- **Increased die tier:** Effects that increase the dice tier of the effect test can at most increase it to 1D12. After that, each further increase adds +1 to the outcome.

The Gaming Group and Reputation

It is fully possible that the characters in the same party will have different reputations, depending on if they brag about their deeds, have bards sing to their glory – or do the opposite, try to keep their involvement secret and actively strive to hide their achievements.

Weapons and Armor

MANY DIFFERENT TYPES of weapons and armor exist in Ambria and Davokar, some of them imported from far-away lands, other locally made but still uncommon. The same goes for other kinds of equipment, as the expanding wealth of Ambria brings new goods into the realm and further into Davokar in the hands of eager fortune hunters.

Weapons

ALCHEMICAL FIRETUBE, PORTABLE
Quality: Flaming, Area Effect (cone)
The portable alchemical firetube is a lighter version of the stationary siege weapon with the same name. The portable version is made of a solid pipe, which is loaded with alchemical flammables that when ignited turn the weapon into a flamethrower. The firetube flames can hit all enemies in front of the carrier; one test is made for each target. Those who are hit suffer full damage, plus damage from fire as an ongoing effect; those who manage to defend themselves suffer half damage and no ongoing effect from fire.

Anyone can use an alchemical firetube, but users who do not have the ability *Siege Expert* at adept level are at risk of triggering a catastrophic failure. For more details, see the rules on Alchemical Weapons on page 98.

A portable firetube used in melee combat counts as a Warhammer.

ALCHEMICAL FIRETUBE, STATIONARY
Quality: Flaming, Unwieldy, Area Effect (cone)
The stationary firetube consists of a cylinder – usually a hollowed log, but fully cast versions also exist – which is loaded with alchemical flammables that when ignited turn the weapon into a devastating flamethrower. The flames can hit all enemies in front of the device; one test is made for each target. Those who are hit suffer full damage, plus damage from fire as an ongoing effect; those who manage to defend themselves suffer half damage and no ongoing effect from fire.

Only persons with the ability *Siege Expert* at adept level can operate a stationary alchemical firetube (see Alchemical Weapons, page 98).

Table 13: Melee Weapons

WEAPON	DAMAGE	QUALITY	COST
Single-handed Weapon	**1D8**		**5 thaler**
Bastard Sword		Bastard Weapon	50 thaler
Fencing Sword		Precise	25 thaler
Crow's Beak	1D8+1	Deep Impact	25 thaler
Lance (on horse)		Bastard Weapon, Long	15 thaler
Flail		Jointed	25 thaler
Long-hammer, one hand grip		Bastard Weapon, Unwieldy	50 thaler
Long-Whip	1D6	Jointed, Ensnaring, Blunt	10 thaler
Estoc	1D8+1	Deep Impact	25 thaler
Short Weapons	**1D6**	**Short**	**1 thaler**
Assassin's Blade		Concealed	5 thaler
Parrying Dagger		Balanced	5 thaler
Stiletto	1D6+1	Deep Impact	5 thaler
Long Weapons	**1D8**	**Long**	**3 thaler**
Halberd	**1D8+1**	Deep Impact	15 thaler
Pike		Precise	15 thaler
Quarterstaff	1D6	Blunt	1 shilling
Chain Staff		Ensnaring	15 thaler
Lance, two-handed grip		Bastard Weapon, Long, Precise	15 thaler
Unarmed Attack	**1D4**	**Short**	**—**
Battle Claw	1D4+1	Deep Impact	1 thaler
Shield			3 thaler
Buckler		Flexible	15 thaler
Steel Shield		Balanced	15 thaler
Heavy Weapons	**1D10**		**10 thaler**
Bastard Sword, two-handed grip		Bastard Weapon, Precise	50 thaler
Double-axe	1D10+1	Deep Impact	50 thaler
Battle Flail		Jointed	50 thaler
Executioner's Axe	1D10+1	Deep Impact, Massive, Unwieldy	50 thaler
Warhammer		Blood-letting, Massive, Unwieldy	50 thaler
Long-hammer, two-handed grip		Bastard Weapon, Massive, Unwieldy, Precise	50 thaler
Executioner's Sword		Precise, Massive, Unwieldy	50 thaler
Heavy Flail		Jointed, Massive, Unwieldy	50 thaler
Grappling Axe	1D10+1	Bastard Weapon, Deep Impact, Unwieldy, Precise	50 thaler

Untrained Use of Alchemical Weapons

The alchemical weapons which may be used by anyone entail a measure of risk for the untrained – a success test with the outcome 20 (or, if used against the characters, a defense test with the outcome 1) means that the weapon detonates in the hands of the user. If this happens the user takes full damage without rolling for *Defense*. Also, all in direct contact with the user must roll *Defense* for half damage. Trained users do not risk such catastrophic failures.

ALCHEMICAL GRENADE

Quality: Flaming, Area Effect (radius)

The alchemical grenade is the smaller cousin of the breaching pot – a sturdy ceramic vessel is filled with volatile substances that explode when ignited with a fuse or when the vessel is crushed. The grenade is fist-sized and is thrown by hand or with a sling.

The thrower aims at one target and may also roll to hit anyone within melee range from the targeted creature. With a successful attack roll, those who are hit suffer full damage, plus damage from fire as an ongoing effect. Should the attack test instead fail, all who manage to defend themselves suffer only half damage and no ongoing effect from fire.

Anyone can use an alchemical grenade, but an untrained user (i.e. who has not learned *Alchemy, Siege Expert* or *Pyrotechnics*) are at risk of triggering a catastrophic failure (see Alchemical Weapons, page 98).

ARROWS AND BOLTS

Besides regular bolts and arrows, a number of special projectiles have been developed. It is not unusual for Ambrian archers to carry two quivers, one with regular arrows and another with a collection of specialized ones.

Precision Arrow

An arrow (or bolt) with the quality Precise, which is especially well-balanced, making it easier to hit the mark.

Flame Arrow

A projectile with an ignitable head. It is often used to set fire to the target, whether it be a living creature, a building or a field of grain (see the quality Flaming for details).

Snaring Arrow

A barbed arrowhead and a thin silk thread attached to the arrow make it possible to ensnare a target using this projectile.

Pulling it out takes a movement action and requires a passed *[Strong –Damage]* test; if successful the target suffers 1D4 damage but the arrow is out. Moving around with a snaring arrow imbedded in one's flesh deals 1 damage per turn, ignoring armor.

Hammer Head

The ball-shaped head of this arrow is meant to stun, rather than damage, the target. After a successful hit, damage is rolled as usual, but the outcome is used to decide if the target is stunned *[Strong –Damage]*. If the target is stunned, he or she may not perform any kind of actions in the following turn.

Armor-piercing Head

This projectile has a head which makes it easier to punch through armor. It has the quality Deep Impact on targets with 1+ in *Armor* value.

Rope Cutter

A Y-shaped tip makes it possible to cut ropes. Hitting the rope is difficult (–5 on the attack test), but a success means that the rope is cut.

Swallow's Tail

The head of this projectile is wide and meant to cause bleeding wounds. The downside is that it is less effective against armored targets. Targets get a +1D4 *Armor* bonus against the Swallow's Tail, but if damaged he or she will bleed like described in the quality Blood-letting.

Whistler

The arrow whistles while flying, as a signal to allies.

Grappling Hook

The arrow sends a grappling hook flying a maximum of ten vertical meters or thirty horizontal meters. A thin silk thread makes it possible to hoist a sturdier rope up to the grappling hook, and once this rope is latched onto the hook it can be used for climbing.

ASSASSIN'S BLADE

Quality: Concealed, Short

The slender grip and the thin feather steel of the blade makes the Assassin's Blade easy to conceal without sacrificing its bite. It is easily strapped to the wrist or ankle, or even attached behind the neck with a lump of resin. Special girdles or hidden pockets in clothes work just as well. The weapon can be smuggled past guards, to be used on secret missions or to be handed over to a prisoner.

BALLISTA

Quality: Massive, Unwieldy

Essentially, the ballista is a massive, stationary crossbow, intended to fire at fixed targets, troop formations on the field and monsters of the most robust sort.

In The Great War, the ballista was used against the undead draft beasts of the Dark Lords, with the intent of stopping their siege towers from reaching the ramparts. This continued during the colonization of Ambria, with the tame beasts of the barbarian warlords as the primary targets. Even today, ballistae are aimed towards Davokar from atop outposts and wall-towers

Table 14: Ranged Weapons

WEAPON	DAMAGE	QUALITY	COST
Ranged Weapon			
Alchemical Firetube	1D12	Flaming, Area Effect (cone)	10 thaler
1 firetube charge			1 thaler
Blowpipe		Special	2 thaler
Crossbow	1D10		8 thaler
Arbalest	1D10+1	Deep Impact	40 thaler
Small Crossbow		Concealed	40 thaler
Repeating Crossbow		Special	40 thaler
Bow	1D8		5 thaler
Longbow		Precise	25 thaler
Horseman's Longbow		Precise	50 thaler
Composite Bow	1D8+1	Deep Impact	25 thaler
10 regular arrows or bolts			1 thaler
Precision Arrow		Precise	5 shillings
Flame Arrow		Flaming	5 shillings
Snaring Arrow		Special	5 shillings
Hammer Head		Special	5 shillings
Armor-piercing Head	+1	Deep Impact	5 shillings
Rope Cutter		Special	5 shillings
Swallow's Tail		Blood-letting	5 shillings
Whistler		Special	2 shillings
Grappling Hook		Special	5 shillings
Throwing Weapon	**1D6**		**2 thaler**
Alchemical Grenade	1D10	Flaming, Area Effect (radius)	1 thaler
Bolas		Special	2 thaler
Throwing Wing		Returning	10 thaler
Spear Sling	1D6+1	Deep Impact	10 thaler

Table 15: Siege Weapons

SIEGE WEAPON	DAMAGE	QUALITY	COST
Alchemical Firetube, stationary	1D12	Flaming, Unwieldy, Area Effect	250 thaler
Ballista	1D12	Massive, Unwieldy	50 thaler
Breaching Pot (buried)	1D12	Wrecking	100 thaler
Breaching Pot (on ground)	1D12	Flaming, Area Effect	100 thaler
Catapult	1D12	Wrecking or Flaming, Area Effect (radius), Unwieldy	250 thaler +50 per Breaching Pot
Missile Battery	1D10	Flaming, Area Effect (radius)	200 thaler +50 per charge
Trebuchet	1D12	Massive, Unwieldy, Wrecking	1250 thaler

BLOWPIPE

Quality: Special

The purpose of the blowpipe is to fire a poisoned dart towards a target. The dart deals no damage itself, but penetrates any protection if rolling higher than the target's *Armor* value with 1D8 (1D10 with the ability *Marksman*).

BOLAS

Quality: Special

A bolas is used in Davokar when someone wants to capture the prey alive; or in order to slow down a target before moving in for the kill.

The bolas is made of two or more weights tied together with ropes. It is aimed at the target's legs or arms in order to hinder movement. Normally, it is thrown at the legs and the attack test is *[Accurate←Quick]*; if the test succeeds, the target cannot move. It is harder to hit the arms of the target – this requires a passed *[Accurate←Quick+3]* and if successful the target has a second chance to fail all success test involving the use of the arms. Removing the bolas counts as a combat action and requires a passed *Quick* test.

BREACHING POT

Quality: Wrecking (if buried) or Flaming, Area Effect (radius)

The breaching pot is a jar filled with volatile substances that explode when ignited or crushed. If the breaching pot has been buried close to a structure it has the quality Wrecking; if it detonates in open air, it has an Area Effect instead. Note that whoever sets off a breaching pot must use a fuse to avoid suffering from the effect.

Anyone can use a breaching pot but only those with the ability *Siege Expert* or *Pyrotechnics* can do so without risking a catastrophic failure. See the rules on Alchemical Weapons on page 98.

Breaching pots can also be used as ammunition for catapults, in which case they have an Area Effect on impact.

CATAPULT

Quality: Wrecking or Burning, Area Effect (radius), Unwieldy

Ballistic devices have long been employed in Alberetor's many wars, and most frequently used, then and now, is the catapult. Compared to its bigger cousin, the trebuchet, it is relatively easy to transport but still very effective against both structures and troops.

It takes someone with the ability *Siege Expert* to load, aim and fire a catapult; it can be loaded with boulders or with breaching pots, the former crushing buildings and the latter more effective against weaker but flammable targets, including hostile troop formations on the field of battle.

CHAIN STAFF

Quality: Long, Ensnaring

The chain staff was developed by elves and has been adopted by some barbarian clans. The weapon is composed of a staff with a short chain attached to each end, making it possible to use the weapon to ensnare a target. The chains often end in a weight or a short blade, making it even more deadly.

COMPOSITE BOW

Quality: Deep Impact

Among the wagon-riding Varaks and Saars who live on the plains west of Davokar, bow-making is a highly esteemed art form. The composite bow is made from layers of horn and sinews over a wooden core; it is shorter and not as precise as the longbow but more powerful. Its size makes it perfect for use while on horseback, the driver's seat or the narrow platform of a battle chariot.

ESTOC

Quality: Deep Impact

The Estoc is a fencing sword but with a tapered blade that ends in a wedge-shaped tip, intended to penetrate the target's armor.

EXECUTIONER'S SWORD

Quality: Precise, Massive, Unwieldy

This giant sword is used by executioners to end the lives of nobles – the axe is for merchants and artisans, the rope for commoners – but there are also those who wield the weapon on the battlefield.

GRAPPLING AXE

Quality: Bastard Weapon, Deep Impact, Precise , Unwieldy

This long-shafted axe is a bastard weapon used during assaults. It can be held one-handed, together with a shield, or alone when climbing ladders to the battlement where it is gripped in both hands to clear the top of the wall. Older models from The Great War were used in sea battles and have a grappling hook on the back of the axe head, in order to secure safe passage from one ship to another.

HEAVY FLAIL

Quality: Jointed, Massive, Unwieldy

The heavy flail is a larger version of the battle flail. As might be expected, the heavier flail is slower but has a greater impact on the unfortunates who are hit by its massive head.

HORSEMAN'S BOW

Quality: Precise

During The Great War the need for a powerful bow that could be used by mounted warriors arose. The traditional longbow was too ungainly – it was so long that it interfered with the horse, or vice versa. To solve this, the asymmetrical horseman's bow was developed.

The lower limb of the bow is shorter than the upper, allowing the bow to be maneuvered back and forth over the horse's back without losing any of its punch. The weapon is tilted forward when it is aimed and fired, in order to maintain equal tension between the two limbs.

In Ambria, the horseman's bow is primarily used in the west, against the forays of the wagon riding Saars. There, the traditional longbow companies are used as defensive troops, but in order to hunt the plunderers down riders are needed, preferably armed with bows.

LANCE

Quality: Bastard Weapon, Long (Precise)

The value of the lance should not be underestimated – the largest monstrosities of the Dark Lords were often slain by lances in the hands of brave knights. The weapon was also used by the Ambrian cavalry to gain dominance over the lowlands and drive barbarians, packs of predators and abominations into the forest of Davokar.

The lance is an elongated spear, with a grip and quillon adapted for use on horseback. When riding a horse the lance has the quality Long, even if gripped in one hand. On foot, the lance is too long to be wielded in only one hand.

LONG-HAMMER

Quality: Bastard Weapon (Massive, Precise, Unwieldy)

The mighty Long-hammer can be used in one hand together with a shield but will – like all bastard weapons – come into its own only when held in a two-handed grip.

LONG-WHIP

Quality: Jointed, Ensnaring, Blunt

The long-whip has been adapted from the common herding or slave-driving whip; its function is not only to drive but also to snare the target. Also, its length gives it a considerable flicking power able to wound lightly armored targets.

MISSILE BATTERY

Quality: Flaming, Area Effect (radius)

The missile battery is a siege weapon unsuitable for use by anyone but trained sappers. It consists of a wooden frame into which hundreds of alchemical missiles can be loaded. When ignited, the burning, screeching missiles rain down on the enemy troops. Every creature caught in the rain of missiles must pass a *Defense* test or get hit by a flaming arrow. If hit, the target rolls again, until a *Defense* test succeeds – then he or she is not hit by any additional arrows.

REPEATING CROSSBOW

Quality: Special

The repeating crossbow is a mechanically advanced version of the crossbow. The weapon has a push lever underneath, for quicker reloading. Only the most skilled blacksmiths are able to construct such technically advanced weaponry. A repeating crossbow is reloaded as a free action, without losing the striking power of the regular crossbow.

SMALL CROSSBOW

Quality: Concealed

Among the thieves and gangs of Yndaros, a smaller and easily concealed version of the crossbow is used. It can be held and fired in one hand, but requires two to load and has the same punch as the standard crossbow. Assassins often apply poison to the bolts, making the weapon very effective for its size.

THROWING WING

Quality: Returning

The throwing wing is designed so that a skilled user can make it return to the place from which it was thrown, if it misses its target (requires a passed *Accurate* test, made as a Free Action). In the depths of Davokar, throwing wings made from hardened wood are used to hunt small game, while the ones used in combat have a knife-sharp edge of steel all around the wing.

TREBUCHET

Quality: Massive, Unwieldy, Wrecking

The queen of siege weapons is the mighty trebuchet, a ballistic device with power enough to raze the sturdiest walls, at least after a number of shots. The trebuchet can only be handled by someone with the ability *Siege Expert* at adept level.

WARHAMMER

Quality: Blood-letting, Massive, Unwieldy

Warhammer is the collective name for a series of two-handed weapons of considerable weight and length. In most cases they are actual hammers, often with long spikes on the hitting surface of the hammer head. Another member of the Warhammer family is the portable alchemical firetube, when used as a melee weapon.

Armor

BELOW ARE DESCRIPTIONS of new types of armor for the characters to protect themselves with.

CONCEALED ARMOR
Type: Light
Quality: Concealed, Flexible
Sorcerers have many reasons to stay hidden. To do this, they often weave mystically reinforced threads into their cloths, resulting in tunics and capes that look ordinary but offer protection. Other groups, such as spies, would love to have access to such garments, so they can avoid unwanted attention while still being ready for battle.

DOUBLE CHAINMAIL
Type: Medium
Quality: Reinforced, Flexible
Double-threaded chainmail can only be crafted by the most skilled blacksmiths; with thinner rings that interlock in layers they craft an armor which is as flexible as chainmail but even more durable.

FIELD ARMOR
Type: Heavy
Quality: Reinforced
Field armor is a full plate forged with pleated sheets, making it less flexible than full plate, but even more impervious to slashing strikes and blows.

FIELD ARMOR OF THE PANSARS
Type: Heavy
Quality: Reinforced, Flexible
The master smiths working for the Pansars can forge full plate armor using pleated steel sheets while retaining the flexibility of standard plated armor.

LAMINATED ARMOR
Type: Medium
Quality: Reinforced
Laminated armor is an older armor-type, nowadays often replaced by the cheaper scale mail or the flexible chain mail. However, some old laminated sets of armor are still around and there are blacksmiths who actually prefer them because of their greater protective capability. Some of Ambria's noble houses still dress in this type of armor, for sentimental... or, as they claim, "traditional" reasons.

Laminated armor can only protect the torso, shoulders and hips – arms and legs are usually dressed in studded leather to maintain mobility.

SKALD'S CUIRASS
Type: Light
Quality: Reinforced, Flexible
Troll singers are often warrior poets and many carry a flexible armor of woven cloth- or leather-strips, strengthened with protective harmonies. The Skald's Cuirass is durable without hampering the wearers' movement, making it popular among other groups as well. For instance, wealthy duelists in Yndaros often color their cuirasses in personal colors, so that they can be recognized from afar.

Table 16: Armor

ARMOR	ARMOR VALUE	QUALITY	COST
Light Armor	**1D4**	**Impeding (−2)**	**2 thaler**
Woven Silk		Flexible	10 thaler
Witch Gown		Flexible	10 thaler
Studded Leather	1D4+1	Reinforced	10 thaler
Order Cloak		Flexible	10 thaler
Skald's Cuirass	1D4+1	Reinforced, Flexible	50 thaler
Wolf Skin		Cumbersome	1 thaler
Concealed Armor		Concealed, Flexible	50 thaler
Blessed Robe		Flexible	10 thaler
Medium Armor	**1D6**	**Impeding (−3)**	**5 thaler**
Double Chain Mail	1D6+1	Reinforced, Flexible	125 thaler
Crow Armor		Cumbersome	2 thaler
Lacquered Silk Cuirass		Flexible	25 thaler
Laminated Armor	1D6+1	Reinforced	25 thaler
Heavy Armor	**1D8**	**Impeding (−4)**	**10 thaler**
Field Armor	1D8+1	Reinforced	50 thaler
Full Plate		Flexible	50 thaler
Field Armor of the Pansars	1D8+1	Reinforced, Flexible	250 thaler
Templar Full Plate	1D8 (+1D4)	Hallowed	100 thaler
Wrath Armor		Retributive	100 thaler

TEMPLAR FULL PLATE

Type: Heavy

Quality: Hallowed

The armor of the templars is a full plate forged, blessed and carried by the order's inner circle. This elite among the elite inherit their armor from a predecessor that fell in battle or, more uncommonly, who died a solemn death in their alcove in Templewall. The armor gives its wearer the protection of Prios, through blessings forged into the steel and by the hallowing blood of both enemies and martyrs.

WRATH ARMOR

Type: Heavy

Quality: Retributive

The reinforced chainmail worn by the warriors in the Guard of the Slumbering Wrath has vengeful mystical energies forged into the rings.

The retributive incantations, according to legend created by the huldra Bovosin more than four centuries ago, give the steel its characteristic blood-red shade – as if the warriors just came from the scene of a tough battle, painted in the blood of their enemies.

Qualities

BLACKSMITHS HAVE COME UP with a number of weapons and types of armor with qualities not featured in the *Core Rulebook*. Before reading about the new ones below, remember that if a quality ever conflicts with how an ability operates, the ability always has precedence.

AREA EFFECT

The effect of the weapon affects an area and damages all who happen to be inside it. One test is made for each creature in the area; those who are hit suffer full damage while those who pass the *Defense* test suffer half damage. Ongoing secondary effects only affect those who suffer full damage from the initial effect.

There are two types of Area Effects, radius and cone, and the former exist in two versions: Melee Range and Short.

Melee Range Radius: 1–2 meters, meaning one creature and all others in its direct vicinity – those

Qualities

Area Effect
Balanced
Bastard Weapon
Blood-letting
Concealed
Deep Impact
Ensnaring
Flexible
Impeding
Jointed
Long
Massive
Reinforced
Returning
Screening
Short
Unwieldy
Wrecking

If a Massive weapon is used against a player character, the player instead rolls the armor die twice and the lowest value determines the level of protection.

who are in melee combat with the target or who could be without having to spend a movement action.

Short Radius: 10 meters, meaning all who are within a movement action from the targeted spot on the ground.

Cone: Anyone present in front of the weapon is at risk of being hit when the weapon is fired. If movement by scale is used on a grid, the cone is as wide as the distance from the weapon. At melee range it is 1–2 meters wide, at short range it is approximately 10 meters wide, and at the maximum medium range it is about 20 meters wide.

BASTARD WEAPON

The weapon can be wielded in one or two hands, even if it only comes into its own when both hands are resting on the grip. The bastard weapon loses one or all of its qualities when used single-handed, but can instead be combined with a shield, which may be preferable at times. Another upside is that it can be used while on horseback, wielded in one hand until the rider dismounts and can grip it in two.

BLOOD-LETTING

The weapon causes wounds, open or internal, that bleed at a rate of 1 *Toughness* per turn. The bleeding starts on the turn after a damaging hit and the effect is cumulative: additional damaging hits increase the blood-letting effect by +1. First aid or other kinds of healing will stop the bleeding.

CONCEALED

The item normally goes unnoticed, or is seen as something else than a protection or a weapon. If someone actively examines the owner/carrier, a test against *[Discreet←Vigilant]* is rolled, otherwise it cannot be discovered. Other hidden items can be discovered at first glance with such a test.

ENSNARING

The weapon can be used to snare a target, which is done with a passed *[Accurate←Quick]* test. An ensnared target cannot move and gets a second chance to fail all success tests. Every attempt to get free requires spending a combat action; this forces the attacker to test *[Accurate←Quick]* again in order to keep the target in check.

Ensnaring melee weapons can be used to try to knock a target prone. The attempt counts as a combat action and requires a passed *[Strong←Strong]* to succeed. A fallen target cannot get up until it has been freed from the ensnaring effect.

Also, note that an Ensnaring weapon may be used with the ability *Ensnare* to perform more advanced maneuvers (see page 64).

MASSIVE

The weapon makes other weapons look puny in comparison. The wielder has a second chance at the damage test; the damage die is rolled twice and the higher of the two outcomes is used. Note that this only applies to the damage die of the weapon, not of additional dice from abilities, powers and elixirs.

REINFORCED

The armor is tougher than other armor in the same category (light, medium, heavy), meaning that the wearer may add +1 to his or her armor rolls.

RETURNING

The weapon is designed in a way so that a skilled user can make it return if an attack misses the target. A passed *Accurate* test is required, which counts as a free action.

SCREENING

The shield is so big that it completely obstructs the line of sight in one direction; archers must move sideways to get a clear line of sight. An ally walking directly behind the carrier of the Screening shield receives the same protection as the carrier.

UNWIELDY

The weapon is heavy or unbalanced in a way which makes it more difficult to swing and control during combat. An attack with the weapon requires a full turn; both the combat action and movement action are spent on the attack. In other words, the wielder cannot both attack and move during a single turn, but once he or she is in place it is possible to make an attack every turn.

WRECKING

The weapon is primarily meant to attack buildings, rather than living creatures; its lack of precision makes it all but impossible to aim at individual enemies, leaving it better suited for shots at fortifications or large areas on the battlefield . Its effect on buildings is considerable and multiple hits will likely wreck the structure – a tower collapses, a wall is breached, a gate is blown open to give the attackers a chance to storm the building.

Creatures who happen to be where a Wrecking weapon hits take damage; *Armor* is ignored but a passed *Defense* test halves the damage. Anyone present in or on a building which is destroyed dies or becomes dying if they fail a *Defense* test; if the test is passed, he or she suffers damage instead, ignoring *Armor*. Furthermore, the individual is buried in the rubble and it takes the rest of the scene to get out of the wreckage.

Mystical Qualities

Mystical Qualities

Acid Coated
Bane Weapon
Death Rune
Desecrated
Flaming
Hallowed
Poison Coated
Retributive
Thundering

SOME BLACKSMITHS are so skilled that they can impart mystical qualities into their master crafts, qualities likened to magic and miracles. The following mystical qualities are known, and of course much coveted.

ACID COATED

Ancient forging procedures make every hit potentially corrosive. Each hit with the weapon deals 1D4 extra damage for 1D4 turns. The acidic effect is not added to the normal damage; it is rolled as a separate hit.

Such a weapon is often carried in a special sheath or socket to avoid damaging the owner. In combat, the acid will affect the wielder if the attack roll is 20 and a consecutive roll is higher than the wielders *Accurate* (or the attribute replacing *Accurate* in attacks).

BANE WEAPON

The weapon is forged in hate and hardened with vengeance, aimed at a specific group of creatures: Elves, Winged Creatures, Undead, Humans, Reptiles, Spiders, Abominations, Trolls or Predators (see page 209 in the *Core Rulebook*). In this respect, changelings count as Elves while ogres and goblins count as Trolls. Dwarves are a group in their own right. The Bane Weapon deals +1D4 damage against members of the selected group and also glows softly in their presence, giving a +1 bonus to *Vigilant* when testing to discover that such a creature is in the vicinity.

DEATH RUNE

The weapon is inscribed with life-denying runes that deal 1D4 extra damage against living and not thoroughly corrupt creatures. In the case of undead or other thoroughly corrupt beings, the energies instead heal 1D4 *Toughness*.

DESECRATED

The weapon or armor is forged in black fire and has extra power against untainted creatures. A creature that is wounded must roll 1D20 under its total corruption value, or suffer +1D4 damage. And when someone wearing Desecrated armor is hit by a successful attack, the attacker must roll 1D20 under its total corruption value; if the outcome is equal to or higher, the armor adds +1D4 protection against the attack.

Thoroughly corrupt creatures always pass these tests, while untainted beings (with zero corruption) always fail.

FLAMING

The weapon glows and even sparks before bursting into flames when actively used. The weapon deals damage as usual, but the target starts to burn - dealing 1D4 damage for 1D4 turns, starting the turn after the initial hit. The fire is extinguished if the target uses a whole turn to roll on the ground and passes a *Quick* test.

HALLOWED

The item is forged in hallowed fire and has extra power against corrupt creatures. A creature that is wounded must roll 1D20 over its total corruption value, or suffer +1D4 damage. When someone wearing Hallowed armor is hit by a successful attack, the attacker must roll 1D20 over its total corruption value; if the outcome is equal to or lower, the armor adds +1D4 protection against the attack.

Thoroughly corrupt creatures always fail these tests, while beings with zero corruption always pass.

POISON COATED

Ancient forging procedures make each hit potentially poisonous. When an attack damages the target it also suffers 1D4 damage for 1D4 turns from poison.

RETRIBUTIVE

The armor is crafted with secret and retributive techniques that cause it to ooze acid. With each hit in melee combat, the attacker must pass a *Quick* test. If failed, the attacker is hit by an acid splash that deals 1D4 damage for 1D4 turns.

THUNDERING

The weapon is instilled with storming, thunderous energies. Each hit echoes with the powers of lightning and deals 1D8 damage, rolled separately from the normal damage caused by the attack. Abilities do not add to this extra damage effect. If any of the damage from this quality penetrates the armor the target also has to pass a *Strong* test or lose an action because of the force unleashed by the Thundering hit.

Ranomar of Vajvod

Ambrian have several master blacksmiths, as for instance the still active Petrona Steelspouse who crafted the lances and sword of King Ynedar. But at the moment, the nobles seem to think that the Vajvod Ranomar is the best smith in the region – at least if judging by the prices they are willing to pay to be able to hang one of his fencing swords from their belts.

Equipment

HERE YOU WILL FIND descriptions of equipment that the characters may need during their adventures, along with items and services they may require when relaxing and recuperating. The objects and services listed are available in all major settlements in Ambria but can also be manufactured by skilled player characters.

Alchemical Elixirs

THE EXCHANGE OF KNOWLEDGE between alchemists in Ambria and Davokar causes ever more elixirs to become available to the Ambrians. Some drugs can only be purchased on the black market in places like Thistle Hold, since they are illegal or at least so inappropriate that selling (or buying) them will attract attention from the authorities and witchhunters. Among these are all the elixirs that give corruption; both Ambrians and barbarians handle the trade in such decoctions discreetly.

Finding a specific elixir on the black market in Ambria requires a *Cunning* test by someone with the boon *Contacts* (treasure hunter or some similar specialization).

ANTIDOTE CANDLE

When lit, this candle emits fumes that work as an antidote on all around it. A weak antidote candle affects every poisoned creature in the vicinity and reduces the effect of ongoing poisons by one level – a strong poison becomes moderate, a moderate weak and a weak is neutralized. A moderate antidote candle does the same, but with a two level reduction: a strong poison becomes weak while moderate and weak ones are neutralized. Note that this does not affect damage already suffered.

DRONE DEW

Drone Dew is a liquid elixir made from drone spores, also containing accelerants.

A person who ingests a dose of the elixir immediately falls asleep if he or she does not pass a *Strong* test, and stays asleep for an hour or until suffering any damage. If the test is passed, the person is instead dazed, with the effect that he or she is limited to one action per turn and cannot use any active abilities for an hour.

FIRE DYE

Fire dye consists of salts that change the color of any fire they are cast into. If the colors are ascribed a specific meaning known to the user and an allied observer it can be used for signaling over long distances. They are also used for entertainment among the wealthy, and by charlatans to impress commoners.

FLASH POWDER

A finely grained powder that emits a blinding light when thrown. Flash Powder is used with the novice level of the ability *Pyrotechnics*.

HOLY WATER

Holy water, instilled with the light of Prios, can heal wounds and sooth souls. It works as a Herbal Cure with +1 on the effect test (meaning +2 *Toughness* if used without the ability *Medicus*), and it also removes 1 point of temporary corruption.

HOMING ARROW

The alchemist marinates an arrow in homing essences, thereby creating an arrow that flies past other combatants, i.e. it does not require clear line of sight. However, the archer must see some part of the target and must roll a normal attack test in order to successfully hit.

HOMUNCULUS

A seed is planted and one day later a miniature servant sprouts from the ground. The homunculus is small as a child, has no abilities and all attribute values are 5 (+5). It serves its maker loyally then withers away after a month; all it leaves behind is a pile of dirt. Creating a homunculus is a true violation of the natural order, meaning that the one using the seed suffers 1D6 temporary corruption.

POISON CANDLE

A seemingly ordinary candle that emits poisonous fumes when lit; revealed with a passed *[Vigilant←alchemist's Discreet]*. The poison is airborne and affects everyone in the room or in the vicinity. The candle must burn for 1D4 turns before the poison is released, so the assassin can light it and leave the room before it takes effect. A weak poison candle deals 2 damage per turn, a moderate 3 damage per turn.

PURPLE SAP

The Purple Sap is made from a decoction of a purple Lily of the Valley, a flower whose cleansing properties and resistance to corruption were discovered by the witches of Davokar long ago. Purchasing the elixir is expensive, because the ingredient is so rare and few alchemists are skilled enough to brew it. The elixir has no effect on permanent corruption or on blight-marks which have already appeared on the user.

Weak: A novice alchemist can brew a potion which immediately removes 1D4 temporary corruption from the user's soul.

Moderate: When made by an adept, the elixir immediately removes 1D6 temporary corruption.

Strong: The master's version removes 1D8 temporary corruption.

REVEALING LIGHT

A wax candle that when lit makes living creatures (not undead or abominations) glow softly in the dark, making it harder to stay hidden (a second

Table 17: Alchemical Elixirs

ELIXIR	COST	ELIXIR	COST
Antidote		**Poison Candle**	
Weak	1 thaler	Weak	8 thaler
Moderate	2 thaler	Moderate	12 thaler
Strong	3 thaler	Protective Oil	2 thaler
Antidote Candle		**Purple Sap**	
Weak	6 thaler	Weak	4 thaler
Moderate	9 thaler	Moderate	8 thaler
Concentrated Magic	1 thaler	Strong	12 thaler
Choking Spores	2 thaler	Revealing Light	2 thaler
Drone Dew	4 thaler	Shadow Tint	3 thaler *
Elemental Essence	2 thaler	Smoke Bomb	2 thaler
Elixir of Life	12 thaler	Spirit Friend	12 thaler
Eye Drops	2 thaler	Spore Bomb	3 thaler
Fire Dye	1 thaler	Stun Bolt	1 thaler
Flash Powder	1 thaler	Thorn Beasties	4 thaler *
Ghost Candle	2 thaler	Thunder Ball	3 thaler
Herbal Cure	1 thaler	**Transforming Draught ***	
Holy Water	2 thaler	Weak	2 thaler *
Homing Arrow	2 thaler	Moderate	4 thaler *
Homunculus	2 thaler *	Strong	6 thaler *
Poison		Twilight Tincture	12 thaler
Weak	2 thaler	War Paint	2 thaler
Moderate	4 thaler	Way Bread	1 thaler
Strong	6 thaler	Wild Chew	1 thaler
		Wraith Dust	2 thaler

* Black market only

chance to fail tests for sneaking up on someone, or a second chance to pass tests to discover someone sneaking). This affects everyone in the room or the vicinity, including the one who lit the candle.

SHADOW TINT

This horribly sickening elixir was once used by mystics wanting to hide just how close they were to becoming thoroughly corrupt, making it a welcomed addition to all sorcerers' collections of mystical decoctions.

Whomever manages to force down the sludge, distorts his or her shadow for a whole scene, making it appear as if the value in total corruption is 1D6 points lower.

SMOKE BOMB

The smoke bomb is a ceramic vessel that emits dense alchemical smoke when crushed, and it is used with the adept level of the ability *Pyrotechnics*. The smoke fills a room or covers a group of people engaged in melee combat.

SPIRIT FRIEND

The miraculous drug called Spirit Friend is cooked in a cauldron, but it is not the liquid that is bottled, but the vapors. The gray-white smoke is captured in small ceramic jars and inhaled when needed. Spirit Friend gives the user level I in the trait *Spirit Form*. The effect lasts for 1D4 turns, to the price of as many points in temporary corruption.

STUN BOLT

The alchemist covers a crossbow bolt in a fast acting muscle relaxant; anyone hit by the bolt must pass a *[Strong –Damage]* test or fall to the ground. The monstrous trait *Robust* gives +2 in *Strong* per level when rolling this test.

THORN BEASTIES

A handful of seeds are thrown to the ground and one turn later 1D4 thorn beasties appear to serve the user. The thorn beasties are small, vaguely humanoid creatures made of thorns; they do not speak but squeak and crack as twigs that are bent and rubbed together. The beasties live during a single scene before drying up to look like thorny witch dolls.

The summoning of the thorn beasties is a clear violation of the natural order, meaning that the one using the seeds suffers 1D6 temporary corruption.

THUNDER BALL

An alchemical load that is thrown and detonates amidst a sudden, loud flash, used with the master level of the ability *Pyrotechnics*.

TRANSFORMING DRAUGHT

This is a powerful mutagen which transforms the body of the user in a monstrous way. During a scene the user is twisted into a bestial half-creature and has a second chance to fail all *Persuasive* tests until the effect wears off.

The draught gives the user a monstrous trait for the rest of the scene; the level of the trait is decided by the strength of the elixir. In addition, each dose consumed deals temporary corruption, also determined by the strength of the elixir. Of course, the physical transformation and the corrupting effect

is reason enough for the elixir to be banned and only available on Ambria's black market.

The following monstrous traits can be acquired, decided by the alchemist when brewing the elixir: *Armored, Natural Weapon, Robust* and *Wings*.

Weak: The draught gives the selected trait at level I, to the cost of 1D4 temporary corruption.

Moderate: The draught gives the selected trait at level II, to the cost of 1D6 temporary corruption.

Strong: The draught gives the selected trait at level III, to the cost of 1D8 temporary corruption.

TWILIGHT TINCTURE

This is an extract of dried stems and leaves from the extremely rare Twilight Thistle. Up until recently the rareness of the herb (on occasion, one or a couple of stems can be found among other offerings in the ruins of Davokar, rather than an actual growing site) coupled with its moderate medical effect made it not very sought-after; it seems to have an effect on certain types of eczema and possibly also on senility if consumed.

However, with the aging of the queen mother has come an increased demand from the court. Of course, the tale of how Lasifor Nightpitch bought the land on which Thistle Hold is built for an armful of Twilight Thistles gave the herb a hefty boost in popularity among fortune hunters.

Lately, the twilight tincture has found another group of users, and a new area of use: it has proven capable of disguising a number of symptoms gained from being undead. Desperate unfortunates – some of them alchemists – searched for ways to hide their death marks, and someone discovered that the twilight tincture (consumed, not smeared on the skin) temporarily made an undead body come to life: the skin regained its redness, the body temperature rose, and the smell of the breath improved dramatically.

The effect lasts for a week per passed *[Strong –permanent corruption]* test. If the test fails, the effect lingers for one more day before dissipating completely. On thoroughly corrupt creatures the effect only lasts for a day per dose, no test is made.

Master Hide

During year 7, the alchemy master Hide is said to have started experimenting with the transformation draught of the witches. He wanted to fly out to meet his Queen on his own wings; instead he became blight-born and was killed before Korinthia reached Yndaros.

THORN BEASTY	
Manner	Rustling and crackling
Race	Creeper
Traits	*Natural Weapon* (I), *Poisonous* (I)
Accurate 13 (−3), **Cunning** 10 (0), **Discreet** 11 (−1), **Persuasive** 5 (+5), **Quick** 15 (−5), **Resolute** 9 (+1), **Strong** 7 (+3), **Vigilant** 10 (0)	
Abilities	None
Weapons	Razor sharp thorns 3
Armor	None
Defense	−5
Toughness 10	**Pain Threshold** 3
Equipment	None
Shadow	Same as the mystic

Tactics: Moves lightning fast with jerky motions towards the appointed goal or task.

WAR PAINT

Mystically charged paints can help a warrior in combat. War paint adds +1 to either *Quick* or *Strong* during an entire scene, and the warrior decides which attribute to boost when the paint is applied.

WILD CHEW

The red chewing resin called Wild Chew is a strong stimulant that makes the chewer more alert, less cautious and much more aggressive. One dose of Wild Chew moves 2 points in *Discreet, Cunning* and *Resolute* to *Quick, Strong* and *Accurate* for the rest of the scene. During the upcoming scene, the user feels weak and has -2 on all attributes.

With time, Wild Chew is highly addictive and severe withdrawal symptoms will occur unless the user consumes one dose each week, with the risk of permanent madness or death. No known drugs can counteract this.

Lesser Artifacts

WITH THE RENAISSANCE of artifact crafting, lesser artifacts have become available for purchase. These items are not necessarily more potent than alchemical elixirs, but are often of a more permanent kind. If a lesser artifact is of a disposable character (like all elixirs are), it will also require that the user has a certain ability. Some lesser artifacts are tightly linked to a mystical tradition or a mystical power and of little use in more general terms, but many of them can be used by anyone and are sure to be a welcomed addition to the tools and equipment of any treasure hunter venturing into Davokar.

Example of Mystical Focus

WITCHCRAFT
Mask made of wood or bone, often painted or adorned with colorful beads

WIZARDRY
Staff carved with power symbols

STAFF MAGIC
Staff head, often a stone entwined in filigree work or held by an ornamental claw

SORCERY
Rod of human bone, engraved with dark runes

SYMBOLISM
A jar filled with air paint

THEURGY
A holy symbol that glows softly in the dark and shines when used

TROLL SINGING
A crumhorn, birch-bark horn or similar instrument that hums or plays quietly even when not used

ANIMAL MASK

Blood wading witches tend to identify with the beasts of the wild, a sentiment embodied by the wearing of animal masks. Every animal mask with mystical properties symbolizes an animal and gives a +1 bonus on an attribute associated with that animal – *Discreet, Quick, Cunning, Strong* or *Vigilant*.

BARK MASK

Green weaving witches often cover their faces with a mask of bark, as a symbol of their connection to nature. Many of these masks are infused with power and provide one re-roll per scene on a test related to plants and anything growing, for example *Thorn Cloak* and *Entangling Vines*. The re-roll may be used for tests to activate such powers or to resist the effect of such powers.

BURIAL SHROUD

The spiritualists among the witches often wear a shroud over their head when contacting the spirits of the dead, since this makes the spirits calmer and allows for a deeper connection. A mystic using such an artifact gains a +1 bonus to *Resolute* in all tests when dealing with spirits – both when trying to control them (as in the power *Tormenting Spirits*) and when trying to resist the effect of monstrous traits used by spirits, involving the *Resolute* attribute.

DEATH MASK

The necromancers' aspiration to dominate death has led to the use of hideous death masks that have been infused with power. A death mask gives a +1 bonus on tests for all powers and rituals affecting the intersection between life and death, for instance the power *Revenant Strike* and the ritual *Raise Undead*.

HEALING SPIDER

A small spider figurine which is placed on an open wound, where it quickly covers itself and the wound in a web that heals 1D12 *Toughness* over the course of a day. The spider cannot heal damage from poison or other internal injuries. When done, the spider creeps up from the wound to be reused on new ones. The one treated by the healing spider suffers one point in temporary corruption.

IRON CROWN

Demonologists often wear a crown of rusty iron when tearing at the world's fabric. These crowns give a +1 bonus when manipulating the world, as with the mystical powers *Exorcize* and *Teleport*, or the ritual *Summon Daemon*.

LUCKY COIN

A gold coin instilled with energies of good fortune. The coin is carried in a pocket and gives a +1 bonus to one success test, once per scene. Whoever toys with such energies is at risk of suffering from the opposite effect; if the outcome of a test modified by the coin is 20, the carrier will have bad luck for the rest of the scene – all success tests have a second chance to fail.

MARLIT CAPE

The skin of a marlit, a reptile known for its sneaky hunting style, is treated with preserving alchemical preparations so that it keeps its camouflaging properties after the death of the beast. The wearer has a +1 bonus to *Discreet* when sneaking and hiding.

MEETING STONE

A stone is loaded with an invitation to a specific person, who upon receiving and touching the artifact instinctively knows where the stone's owner is waiting. Only a mystic (with at least one mystical power) can activate a meeting stone.

MIND PRISM

The illusionists of Ordo Magica often use a prism to describe how the perception of reality may be broken down and understood. Some of these crystals are filled with so much suggestive energies that they provide a +1 bonus to all tests related to the creation of illusions.

MYSTICAL FOCUS

A tradition-specific focus gives a +1 bonus on all tests related to all powers of the tradition, but limited to one use per scene. The bonus may be used together with other lesser artifacts that also provide a bonus to success tests for the mystical power in question. A mystical focus is bound to the user as other, higher artifacts – that is, by spending an experience point or by willingly accepting one point in permanent corruption.

ORDER MEDALLION

The medallions of Ordo Magica are given to novices and stay with the wizards for their entire career. When the wizard reaches adept level, the medallion transforms to symbolize this step; the same thing happens when reaching master level.

Some chapters have made the order medallion mandatory and have also bound certain functions to it, such as the ability to open doors which are closed to outsiders/novices/adepts and to activate the chapter's magic circle.

Table 18: Lesser Artifacts

ARTIFACT	COST
Animal Mask	10 thaler
Bark Mask	10 thaler
Burial Shroud	10 thaler
Death Mask	10 thaler
Healing Spider	4 thaler
Iron Crown	10 thaler
Lucky Coin	8 thaler
Marlit Cape	4 thaler
Meeting Stone	2 thaler
Mind Prism	10 thaler
Mystical Focus	12 thaler
Order Medallion	2 thaler
Pest Mask	8 thaler
Ritual Codex	4 thaler
Ritual Focus	8 thaler
Ritual Seal	12 thaler
Ruler's Ring	10 thaler
Rune Staff	12 thaler
Soul Stone	12 thaler
Spark Stone	10 thaler
Spell Seal	
Novice	8 thaler
Adept	12 thaler
Spell Scroll	
Novice	2 thaler
Adept	4 thaler
Master	6 thaler
Staff Foot	10 thaler
Staff Head	10 thaler
Sun Mask	10 thaler
Toad Guard	1 thaler
Transcendental Weapon	12 thaler
Witch Braid	8 thaler

PEST MASK

In a world full of contagions and poisons it is no wonder that many methods – effective or only superstitious – have been developed to resist such phenomena. The Confessors of the Sun Church, for instance, carry pest masks to protect themselves. They allow the wearer to use their *Resolute* instead of *Strong* on tests to resist sicknesses and poisons.

RITUAL CODEX

A ritual is penned down in a codex so that another ritualist can perform it without having previously learned the ritual. The codex can only be used once.

RITUAL FOCUS

A tradition-specific object which gives a +1 bonus on success tests for all rituals belonging to the tradition. See examples to the right.

RITUAL SEAL

The artifact crafter binds a ritual to a seal; when broken, the effect of the ritual is triggered. The creator of the seal need not know the ritual, but must be in the company of one who does when it is created (or have access to a ritual codex explaining the ritual; the codex is destroyed with this act). He or she who breaks the seal suffers from temporary corruption as usual.

RULER'S RING

Prominent mind-warping wizards often carry a gold ring on a finger, around the wrist or upper arm, or on the head in the form of a headband. To them, this represents the noble endeavor of the ruler. These rings are often instilled with the ability to dominate all living beings. If so, the gold ring gives a +1 bonus to all test involving powers and rituals of *Wizardry* affecting the will of the target, for example the use of, and resistance to, *Bend Will* and *Telepathic Interrogation*.

RUNE STAFF

The hallmark of the staff mage is his or her personal staff, carved with the runes of the elements. In the hand of its owner, the staff emits a protective aura (*Armor* +1D4), and is also the instrument through which the mage wields his or her powers.

SOUL STONE

A Soul Stone is the item required to perform the ritual with the same name.

SPARK STONE

The power of a Pyromancer is increased by this glowing amber. The spark stone is a weaker version of the renowned Sun Stones that the master pyromancers of old could craft from summoned fire spirits. Nowadays, the fire wizards have to make do with lesser artifacts, far from as powerful but still a great help to those whose skills relate to fire and burning. All powers with fire effects gain a +1 bonus to the effect die when used by someone with a spark stone in hand or on top of his or her staff.

Examples of Ritual Focuses

WITCHCRAFT
Clothing in natural fabrics with woven power symbols

WIZARDRY
A collection of metal symbols, where different metals represent different elements or principles

STAFF MAGIC
A staff foot in metal, used to draw symbols on the ground

SORCERY
Chalice shaped like the skull of a daemon, from which sacrificial blood is drunk during the ritual

SYMBOLISM
Rune-carving tools with glowing tips

THEURGY
Shrouding from a lightbringer, carried like a cape or draped over the object of the ritual

TROLL SINGING
Stone tablet, wooden board or bone shield with carved symbols, functioning as a note or song sheet of ancient hymns and powerful rhythms

SPELL SCROLL

Artifact crafters in Ordo Magica can bind a mystical power at the novice, adept or master level (depending on the level of the artifact) to a scroll. The power may then be activated by someone else who has *Wizardry* at a level equal to or higher than the level of the power, or someone who has the ability *Loremaster* at adept level. Whoever activates the scroll suffers temporary corruption as usual and the scroll is spent upon activation.

SPELL SEAL

An artifact crafter has bound a mystical power at the novice or adept level (depending on the level of the artifact) to a seal; when the seal is broken, the power is activated. Whoever breaks the seal suffers temporary corruption as usual and the seal is spent when broken.

STAFF FOOT

A staff foot forged with strengthening spells can give the staff of a staff mage extra power when used as a weapon. The artifact is attached to the staff and gives a +1 bonus on the effect tests of all melee or ranged attacks, and on all powers which directly use the staff as a weapon. Even if this artifact most often is attached to a rune staff, it may be attached to an ordinary wooden staff with the same effect.

STAFF HEAD

A special ornament at the top of the staff mage's staff can provide extra focus. The staff head – often a beautiful stone encased in meteoric iron – gives a +1 bonus to all success tests that do not directly involve the staff as a weapon, as for instance *Blood Storm* and *Sphere*.

SUN MASK

The sun masks of the theurgs bestow spiritual warmth to the cold-hearted and spread light where no other light can reach. Worn by a theurg, they can also assist in combat against undead and abominations. The mask radiates light around the wearer as if it is a torch; also, all powers with holy or banishing effects have a +1 bonus to effect tests.

TOAD GUARD

A figurine in the form of a toad acts as an alarm. The user – who has to know at least one mystical power – whispers a triggering condition to the figurine; the trigger has to be of a physical nature and must occur close to the toad guard, for example that *"someone passes through the grove"* or *"the door is opened from outside."* If activated, the toad will wake everyone with a loud croaking.

TRANSCENDENTAL WEAPON

These weapons were forged to allow a wielder to strike from a distance. Only mystics (defined as someone who has

learned at least one mystical power) know how to use such an artifact.

The attack is rolled as if in melee combat but may hit distant targets and requires a clear line of sight, just as ranged attacks. Active abilities may be used, but at one level lower: a master may use the adept level of the ability through the transcendental weapon; an adept may use the novice level. A novice cannot use the ability together with a transcendental weapon.

WITCH BRAID

This braid is made from three types of hair or fur and keeps death at bay, giving a +1 bonus to *Strong* during death tests. Non-player characters with the braid get to make death tests, with the +1 bonus.

Traps

TRAPS COME in two types, mechanical and alchemical. Mechanical ones can be handled by untrained users, but for the sake of speed and security training in the ability *Trapper* is recommended. When it comes to alchemical mines, *Trapper* or the ability *Pyrotechnics* is a requirement for use.

ALCHEMICAL MINE

Alchemical mines are crafted by an alchemist who possesses the ability *Trapper* and/or *Pyrotechnics*. When triggered, they spray flammable substances over the wretched targets and deal fire damage for a number of turns. To scrape off the flammables requires a combat action and a passed *[Quick←Cunning]* test,

Table 19: Traps

TRAP	COST
Alchemical Mine	
Weak	2 thaler
Moderate	4 thaler
Strong	8 thaler
Mechanical Trap	
Weak	1 thaler
Moderate	2 thaler
Strong	3 thaler

the latter being the mine-maker's attribute value (the average alchemist can be assumed to have *Cunning* 13 (–3)). An alternative is to dive into water, which smothers the fire for as long as you stay there. Allies trying to help the burning target may make separate tests in order to scrape off the substances.

Weak: The explosion deals 1D8 damage, after which the substance keeps burning for 1D4 turns, dealing 1D4 damage per turn.

Moderate: The explosion deals 1D10 damage, after which the substance keeps burning for 1D6 turns, dealing 1D6 damage per turn.

Strong: The explosion deals 1D12 damage, after which the substance keeps burning during 1D8 turns, dealing 1D8 damage per turn.

MECHANICAL TRAP

Mechanical traps come in many designs, but the basic version consists of two jagged semi-circles that slam shut when triggered. A passed *[Strong←Cunning]* test is required to get free, the latter being the trap-makers attribute value (the average trap-maker can be assumed to have *Cunning* 13 (–3)). Each attempt to break free counts as a combat action.

Weak: The trap deals 1D8 damage.
Moderate: The trap deals 1D10 damage.
Strong: The trap deals 1D12 damage.

Tools of the Trade

ARTIFACT CATALOGUE

This well-thumbed copy compiling all the troll smith Xavaundo's knowledge was recorded by Master Balinda of Ordo Magica and gives a +1 bonus to success tests with *Artifact Crafting*.

BESTIARY

A richly illustrated catalogue of the dangers of the world, including marginal notes from previous owners regarding the best ways to avoid monsters – or how to combat them effectively. The bestiary gives a +1 bonus to success tests with *Beast Lore*.

CARTOGRAPHER'S INSTRUMENTS

Writing utensils, parchment, compass, ruler and a sextant are the base instruments of a trained cartographer. Using these tools gives a +1 bonus on all success tests when trying to draw accurate maps.

CHEATING KIT

Weighted dice, marked cards and game pieces give the player character a +1 bonus on all success tests when gambling (see the boon *Cheat* on page 52 for risks on cheating at games).

Lesser Artifacts

NOVICE ARTIFACTS
Healing Spider
Meeting Stone
Order Medallion
Pest Mask
Ritual Codex
Spell Scroll
Toad Guard

ADEPT ARTIFACTS
Animal Mask
Bark Mask
Burial Shroud
Death Mask
Iron Crown
Lucky Coin
Marlit Cape
Mind Prism
Ritual Focus
Ruler's Ring
Spark Stone
Spell Scroll
Spell Seal (novice)
Staff Foot
Staff Head
Sun Mask
Witch Braid

MASTER ARTIFACTS
Mystical Focus
Ritual Seal
Rune Staff
Spell Scroll
Spell Seal (adept)
Soul Stone
Transcendental Weapon

CLIMBING GEAR

A collection of ropes, buckles, hooks and tools used for climbing in difficult terrain. Climbing gear gives a +1 bonus to all success tests for climbing.

DISGUISE KIT

Make-up, wigs and wax for altering facial features is included in the kit, together with an array of basic clothes of local significance. The kit gives a +1 bonus on all success tests when trying to fool someone with a disguise.

EXCAVATION TOOLS

A couple of shovels, a small skewer, a strainer and a bucket, together with brushes, a knotted measuring line and a loupe. Excavation tools give a +1 bonus to finding treasures in the ruins of the world.

FIELD LABORATORY

Burner, retort stand, pipettes, mortar and other instruments needed by an alchemist. The field laboratory gives a +1 bonus to all success tests with *Alchemy*.

FIELD LIBRARY

Half a dozen reference books along with a dozen scrolls on more specialized topics. The field library gives a +1 bonus to all success tests with *Loremaster*.

FIELD SMITHY

The portable field smithy is a must for all traveling blacksmiths. It consists of a collection of tools, a field furnace with a water bath and a small anvil. Anyone using the smithy gains a +1 bonus to success tests with *Blacksmith*.

FIELD SURGEON'S INSTRUMENT KIT

The kit of a field surgeon contains tools to burn, cut and treat wounds and diseases, and gives a +1 bonus on all success tests with the ability *Medicus*.

FORGERY KIT

Aside from a loupe, paper, parchment and a collection of pens and ink, this package includes stamps, seals and pre-printed stationery from a long list of organizations, trading houses and similar. The kit gives the user a +1 bonus on all success tests when trying to fool someone with a forged document.

POISON MANUAL

A manual on the use of poisons, richly illustrated with examples on what to do, and not do, in order to successfully brew decoctions and elixirs. Anyone using the manual gains a +1 bonus on all success tests with Poisoner.

TRAPPER'S MANUAL

A used copy of the famous ogre Crueljaw's lustful tome that contains a lengthy record of traps, from simple mare snares and needle-traps in box lids to massive contraptions suited for a king's burial mound. The book gives a +1 bonus to all success tests with *Trapper*.

Table 20: Tools of the Trade

TOOL	COST
Artifact Catalogue	10 thaler
Bestiary	10 thaler
Cartographer's Instruments	10 thaler
Cheating Kit	10 thaler
Climbing Gear	10 thaler
Disguise Kit	10 thaler
Excavation Tools	10 thaler
Field Laboratory	10 thaler
Field Library	10 thaler
Field Smithy	10 thaler
Field Surgeon's Instrument Kit	10 thaler
Forgery Kit	10 thaler
Poison Manual	10 thaler
Trapper's Manual	10 thaler

Food and Drink

BORED NOBLES, HOMECOMING treasure hunters and scrawny day thalers – they may appear to have nothing in common, but appearances are deceptive: they all know to appreciate a good meal!

Then again, what they regard as a tasty meal, and what they are prepared to pay for it, differs very much between the representatives of these groups.

Below is a list of food dishes, beverages and other types of stimulants. The listed dishes can be found on menus all over Ambria and some of them can also be offered in the settlements of the clans. But the prices listed must be seen as a guideline, since they can vary considerably – Afadir's Triumph Tavern in Thistle Hold requests shining thalers of their customers, but in the Baiags' settlement by the lake Big Mere anyone can get a fantastic meal in exchange for a utility item or a small service.

Table 21: Food and Beverage

DISH	COST
Desserts	
Hack Tray (cheese and meats)	3 shillings
Fried Pastry	2 ortegs
Fruit Pie	1 thaler
Fruit Pudding	1 orteg
Fruit Sherbet	7 thaler
Ice Cream & Fruit	2 ortegs
Honey-roasted Sorrel	3 shillings
Candied Ginger	1 shillings
Marmalade Confectionery	3 shillings
Marzipan Figurines	5 shillings
Nougat Confectionery	2 ortegs
Nuts in Chocolate	1 orteg
Truffle-buttered Biscuit	5 ortegs
Sugar-coated Rose Petals	5 ortegs
Salty-sweet Needles	5 ortegs
Waffles with Butter and Honey	3 shillings
Beverages	
Table Ale (watered stut)	1 orteg
Bottle of Blot (mulled wine)	3 thaler
Bottle of Ludendrink (mulled wine)	2 thaler
Bottle of Red Wine (unspecified)	1 thaler
Bottle of White Wine (unspecified)	1 thaler
Bottle of Southern Slopes (from Alberetor)	15 thaler
Bottle of of Vearra's Red (simple wine)	2 thaler
Can of Vesa	4 ortegs
Tankard Blackbrew (unspecified)	1 orteg
Tankard Stut (unspecified)	3 ortegs
Tankard Adersel (triple fermented ale)	8 shillings
Tankard Argona (fine stut)	2 shillings
Tankard The Duke's Relief (simple stut)	1 shilling
Tankard Kurun's Honor (triple fermented)	5 shillings
Tankard Urtal (triple fermented red ale)	3 shillings
Tankard Veloum (barbarian must)	2 shillings
Tankard Zarekian Blackbrew	1 shilling
Fish	
Fish Sauce & Crispbread	5 ortegs
Trout Pudding with Turnips	15 shillings
Salted Herring with Turnips	5 shillings
Buttered Walleye with Mash	22 shillings

DISH	COST
Porridge	
Watered Porridge	4 ortegs
Ale-porridge with Butter	2 shillings
Spicy Cream-porridge	1 thaler
Meat	
Barbecued Young-boar with Beats	6 shillings
King's Steak in Gravy	8 shillings
Slow-roast with Stewed Carrot	5 shillings
Hash Patties with Turnips	2 shillings
Roka Sausage with Mashed Beats	12 shillings
Stuffed Lung with Black Mash	4 shillings
Pies	
Fish Pie	5 shillings
Offal Pie	4 shillings
Cabbage Pie	1 shilling
Meat Pie	2 shillings
Trout Pie	8 shillings
Kidney Pie	2 shillings
Mushroom Pie	4 shillings
Stews	
Mixed Stew	5 ortegs
Fish & Turnips	1 shilling
Cabbage Stew	3 ortegs
Meat & Beats	8 ortegs
Root Vegetable Stew	4 ortegs
Soups	
Blood-soup with Dark Bread	5 ortegs
Onion Soup with Crispbread	4 ortegs
Tea	
Fruit Tea	1 shillings
Iron Oak Tea	8 ortegs
Spice Tea	1 orteg
Smoked Tea	4 ortegs
Herbal Tea	2 ortegs

Beverages

VESA

A mix of buttermilk and goat whey enjoyed by all barbarian clans. Fresh and very tasty, albeit an acquired taste.

BLACKBREW

The rich beer of the clans, ranging in quality from very cheap Brute-brew to the reasonably tasty version brewed by Clan Zarek.

STUT

The most common type of ale in Ambria. Comes in many types and brands, but the most popular and price worthy is brewed by House Argona.

VELOUM

A brighter kind of beer, common among the clans north of Karvosti. Weaker than blackbrew but just as rich and with more flavor.

BRUTEBREW

Hard alcohol mixed with spiced water, so disgusting that the barbarians never drink it other than in connection with bets or special rituals.

Food Cultures

The food cultures of the clans and the Ambrians are varied, but generally the Ambrians prefer processed dishes (brawns, sausages, pâtés, etc.) while the barbarian dishes are more rustic, such as stews and barbecues.

Musical Instruments

MUSIC IS A VITAL component in all cultures of the Davokar region. Here is a list of some of the most popular musical instruments.

BAGPIPE
A flute is attached to a leather bag which functions as a bellow. This instrument is particularly popular among some of the clans, but versions of it can also be found across the Ambrian countryside. However, it is never seen in Ambria's finer salons...

BRASS HORN
A decent bellowing instrument for pompous situations.

BIRCH-BARK HORN
Commoners in the Ambrian countryside use these horns for multiple purposes, but mainly to scare away beasts and call on their livestock. The horn is also used to send messages over long distances; a lone herdsman can signal surrounding shielings from where the message is passed on. Skilled horn-blowers actually play in a unique way, so that everyone knows who is sending the message: *"here be baiagorn tracks," "a cow is missing"* or *"goblins have stolen my cheese."*

DRUM
A rhythm instrument that comes in many forms, from the simpler drums heard among the clans of Davokar, to the metal-framed instruments of the Ambrian army.

FIDDLE
An often three-stringed instrument, played with a bow made from horsehair, very common among peasants in Ambria.

FLUTE
There are innumerable kinds of flutes, from slender metal flutes to wind instruments made from reeds, tree branches and horn. Other known types are the panpipe and the shawm, the latter identified by its shrill tone.

HURDY-GURDY
The hurdy-gurdy is a string-instrument with a crank handle that gives rise to a creaking sound to rhythmically accompany the music. It has long been popular in Ambria (and Alberetor before

Table 22: Musical Instruments

INSTRUMENT	COST
Bagpipe	1 thaler
Birch-bark Horn	1 shillings
Brass Horn	1 thaler
Drum	3 shillings
Fiddle	3 thaler
Flute	2 shillings
Hurdy-gurdy	3 thaler
Lute	15 shillings
Mouth Harp	5 shillings
Shawm	5 shillings
Spinet	15 thaler

that), but in Yndaros it has come to be associated with beggars. Many refugees from the south earn their living by constantly exposing those passing by to a cacophony of melodic droning, creaking and grinding.

LUTE
String-instrument with a pear-shaped base, played with the fingers or a pick.

MOUTH HARP
The tiny mouth harp is carried by many daythalers, entertainers and jesters, and its sound can often be heard in the background at gatherings in Ambria's simpler environments.

SPINET
The spinet is a fingerboard instrument which is popular in the court of Yndaros and forms the backbone of Ambrian Court Music, together with the lute.

Trade Goods

TRADE IS THE LIFE-BLOOD of Ambria and much of it goes on in Davokar as well. Goods do not always have a practical use; instead they are the basis for different type of craft items.

Tobacco

MANY AMBRIANS ENJOY a good smoke, almost as much as a sturdy drink or a shocking tall-tale. After a meal, during work, after work or instead of work – any time is a great time for a stopping of tobacco!

Table 23: Trade Goods

GOODS	VALUE
Cotton Fabric, one roll	1 thaler
Gold, one bar	500 thaler
Turmeric, one box	1 orteg
Honey, one jar	1 shilling
Ginger, one box	5 ortegs
Iron, one bar	1 thaler
Cinnamon, one box	1 thaler
Cardamom, one box	5 ortegs
Copper, one bar	5 shillings
Clove, one box	7 ortegs
Spices, one box	3 ortegs
Cumin, one box	5 ortegs
Roka Berries, one box	12 ortegs
Mint, one box	5 ortegs
Oil (vegetable), one earthen	5 ortegs
Saffron, one box	50 thaler
Salt, one sack	1 shillings
Silk, one roll	50 thaler
Silver, one bar	50 thaler
Sugar, one sack	1 thaler
Grain, one sack	2 shillings
Tar, one barrel	5 shillings
Vinegar, one earthen	1 shilling

Table 24: Tobacco utensils

UTENSIL	COST
Clay Pipe	3 shillings
Long-stemmed Seafoam Pipe	1 thaler
Wooden Pipe	5 shillings
Smoke Tube	5 ortegs
Snuff Box	1 shilling

Table 25: Tobacco Types

TYPE	COST
Fruit Tobacco, one box	4 ortegs
Smelling Snuff, one box	2 thaler
Longbottom Leaf, one box	8 shillings
Chewing Tobacco, one box	6 ortegs
Herbal Tobacco, one box	2 shillings

Measures in Ambria

Trade goods are often transported in the following volumes and weights in Ambria:

Box	0,1 kg
Pound	½ kg
Bar	1 kg
Roll	5 kg
Bale	20 kg
Tankard	½ liter
Jar	1 liter
Earthen	5 liter
Keg	10 liter
Sack	20 liter
Barrel	200 liter

INDEX

PLAYER

NAME

RACE

OCCUPATION

PAIN THRESHOLD

TOUGHNESS
MAXIMUM

CORRUPTION
PERMANENT

CORRUPTION THRESHOLD

SHADOW

EXPERIENCE

UNSPENT

QUOTE

| ACCURATE | CUNNING | DISCREET | PERSUASIVE | QUICK | RESOLUTE | STRONG | VIGILANT |

ABILITIES, POWERS, BOONS & BURDENS

NAME

EFFECT

TYPE   ◇◇◇ N A M

NAME

EFFECT

TYPE   ◇◇◇ N A M

NAME

EFFECT

TYPE   ◇◇◇ N A M

NAME

EFFECT

TYPE   ◇◇◇ N A M

NAME

EFFECT

TYPE   ◇◇◇ N A M

NAME

EFFECT

TYPE   ◇◇◇ N A M

NAME

EFFECT

TYPE   ◇◇◇ N A M

NAME

EFFECT

TYPE   ◇◇◇ N A M

NAME

EFFECT

TYPE   ◇◇◇ N A M

NAME

EFFECT

TYPE   ◇◇◇ N A M

NAME

EFFECT

TYPE   ◇◇◇ N A M

NAME

EFFECT

TYPE   ◇◇◇ N A M

WEAPONS & ARMOR

WEAPON	DAMAGE	QUALITY	ATTRIBUTE
WEAPON	DAMAGE	QUALITY	ATTRIBUTE
WEAPON	DAMAGE	QUALITY	ATTRIBUTE
WEAPON	DAMAGE	QUALITY	ATTRIBUTE

ARMOR

PROTECTION

QUALITY

ARMOR

PROTECTION

QUALITY

DEFENSE

DEFENSE

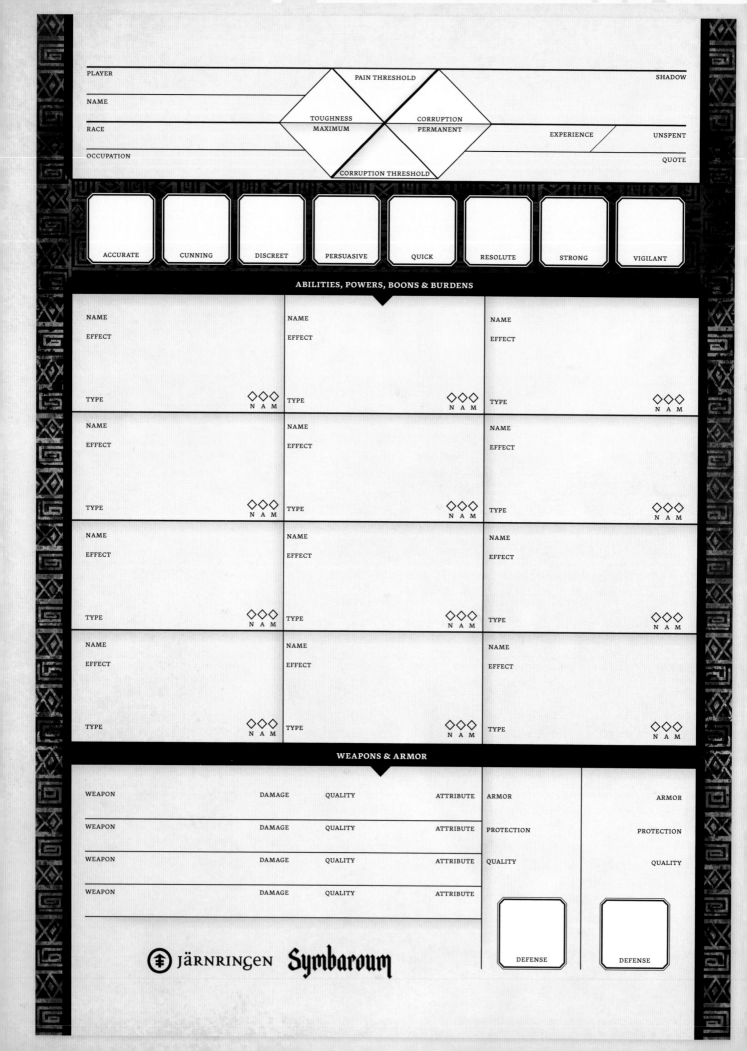

JÄRNRINGEN   Symbaroum

AGE HEIGHT WEIGHT

APPEARANCE

BACKGROUND

PERSONAL GOAL

EQUIPMENT

FRIENDS & COMPANIONS

NAME	RACE	OCCUPATION	PLAYER
NAME	RACE	OCCUPATION	PLAYER
NAME	RACE	OCCUPATION	PLAYER
NAME	RACE	OCCUPATION	PLAYER
NAME	RACE	OCCUPATION	PLAYER

GROUP NAME

GROUP GOAL

ARTIFACTS & MYSTICAL TREASURES

NAME	POWERS	CORRUPTION
NAME	POWERS	CORRUPTION
NAME	POWERS	CORRUPTION
NAME	POWERS	CORRUPTION

MONEY

OTHER ASSETS